The Thr
Miracle
Mandate

Receive God's Blessings
Release His Power

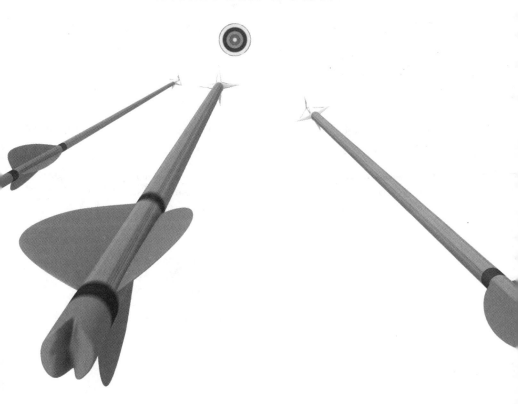

Rob Cresswell

The Threefold Miracle Mandate

ISBN 13: 9780957264236
ISBN 10: 0957264232

Published by FiftyFive Eleven Ltd

Printed in the USA

This book is available from
www.SpiritLifestyle.com

"In this thought provoking and insightful book Rob Cresswell delves into the deep connection between the fall of Adam and the victory of Christ. Through this masterful work you will learn how to activate the threefold blessing of the cross and experience the riches of God's provision and release the supernatural authority that Christ has given His church. You will be challenged. You will be changed!"

Dr. Kynan Bridges
Bestselling author, Possessing Your Healing
Senior Pastor Grace and Peace Global Fellowship

"Over the years that I have known Rob and Aliss, I have watched first-hand their incredible devotion to the Lord and the manifestation of His kingdom on the earth through the supernatural demonstration of God's Spirit. Rob's book, "The Threefold Miracle Mandate" captures the essence of the last day commission of the church on planet earth as the fullness of God is demonstrated to the lost. In it, Rob clearly captures incredible biblical and practical truth dealing with the Lord's provision for us along with our complete redemption, spirit soul and body. More importantly, it captures our need to demonstrate a gospel of power to a lost generation that will be transformed by the revelation of Jesus Christ. I believe this book will bless many and help prepare an overcoming army to manifest God's kingdom."

Paul Keith Davis
WhiteDove Ministries

"Rob Cresswell has written an engaging book that will stir you to believe God for the impossible and draw you into a deeper relationship with Jesus. He and Aliss have lived remarkable lives of obedience that have been blessed with a remarkable anointing for the miraculous. The stories and teaching contained in The Threefold Miracle Mandate impart faith for and understanding of the supernatural ways of God."

Justin Perry
Lead Pastor, MorningStar Fellowship Church

Contents:

FOREWORD
by Aliss Cresswell

The first time I heard my husband Rob teach on the revelation contained in this book was at one of our 'School of the Spirit' meetings. I was moved to tears. I've heard him share it a few times since, and each time, scores of people are so impacted, they come and ask where they can get hold of the teaching. Well, let me tell you that you're blessed because you're holding it in your hands! I believe this revelation has the power to change your life.

What made me cry is this: After contending for years to see the miraculous power of God demonstrated in everyday life, just like I read in the Scriptures, we got breakthrough. It was as if the floodgates had been opened and we saw more miracles than we ever thought possible. Just out and about – in shops, on planes, in homes, at work. Even with atheists, Satanists, and the 'down and out'.

The miracles broke out when we opened our café in 2009 in Chester UK, then continued through our shops and our boutique B&B. These miracles continue to this day, not only through us and our team, but through people like you as well. People who are hungry to see the signs and wonders manifesting in their own lives.

We are using our workshops and training videos to inspire ordinary people to become extraordinary: demonstrating God's love and power in homes, workplaces and everywhere they go. What we want to see is hundreds and thousands of lives changed through powerful encounters with Jesus and communities transformed throughout all society.

In this book, Rob explores just how deep and multi-faceted the power of miracles is. He lays a strong Biblical foundation to all we have witnessed God do. His teaching has helped me understand how the miracles demonstrated by Jesus on earth were not just to show who He is but how and why we can witness miracles in and through our lives today too. True miraculous power convicts people of sin to repentance (see Luke 5:8) and reveals God's glory (see John 2:11).

I have been married to Rob for three decades, and I can personally vouch for his character; his integrity, wisdom, humility, kindness, gentleness and love of God. How he has laid down his life to serve and to search out the depths of God and to understand the Truth. He has a wonderful teaching gift in which he has the ability to unpack what has been said or what is being experienced and to explain what it means in simple terms. This, along with his wisdom has been invaluable to me over the course of our life together, as we have brought up our family and throughout our ministry and businesses. I know that you too will be blessed by his insight as you read this book.

Over the years we have often come across the attitude that miracles are not all that important to the Christian life. This caused Rob to search deep into the Scriptures, and he uncovered some surprising truths. In this book you will discover why miracles are fundamental to our new life in Jesus and how you can receive your inheritance in Christ now, and not just in the future. You'll see that there need be no barrier to you receiving God's blessings and find out how you can release His supernatural, miracle working power everywhere you go.

Rob candidly shares some of our private stories that have never been made public before. You'll read about times where things didn't seem to be going so well in our lives: our struggles, our failures and mistakes. How God spoke to us and tested us. We're sharing these things in the hope that you can see how God uses us despite our weaknesses. So that you too can see, learn, and grow in Him, and can overcome and receive all the blessings gained through the inheritance Jesus purchased for you at the cross. We want you to fulfil your purpose and chase your God-given dreams.

Rob goes on to describe the movement that is steadily growing worldwide and the uprising that is gaining traction. I pray you will be inspired, encouraged, provoked and launched into all that God has created you to be as you apply the powerful teaching in this book to your life.

Our hope is that through this practical Bible study you'll be given keys to moving in the miraculous power of God. We pray that our personal stories, along with application of the word of God to your everyday experience will help you greatly. We have activated people all over the world to step out in faith and demonstrate the power of God and I believe if you read this book with an open heart, pursue the way of love and earnestly desire the things of the Spirit, you can be launched to live the life you've dreamed of, and more besides.

Aliss

www.AlissCresswell.com

Prologue:
John of Greystoke
Transformative Inheritance

"Instead of your shame you will receive a
double portion, and instead of disgrace you
will rejoice in your inheritance." Isaiah 61:7

*T*he jungle is alive with bird call and incessant insect chatter. Far below the leafy canopy, illuminated here and there by bright shafts of morning sunlight, a mist rises from the dark forest bed. A solitary dragonfly darts through an open glade, as all at once an eerie quietness descends on the scene.

Without warning: an explosion of movement. A large dark animal baring teeth, claws and wild eyes. Darting and grasping in panic, the great ape flees for its life before the big cat. Flashing from the shadows, a forest leopard hot on the heels of her quarry.

A riot of noise erupts from the jungle as apes all around let out shrieks of warning and danger. One of their ape colony has been attacked and injured and he is beginning to tire from the chase. The leopard darts after her prey with lithe agility until quite suddenly her quarry stops, dead still. He turns with a puzzling show of surrender, or is it perhaps defiance?

Surprised, the leopard freezes; dropping to her haunches, ears laid back and tail swaying with menace. Bristling, they fix eyes on each other in primal anticipation, transfixed and panting deeply. The next move will be the death strike.

But wait! What is this strange creature flying into the clearing with a blood curdling cry? It collides with the leopard with such force that both roll into the undergrowth in a deadly embrace. A hidden frenzy of feline squealing and grunting, the leaves thrashing and then… silence.

Slowly the strange, victorious beast emerges from the darkness. Its eye is intelligent but menacing as it grimly holds the still warm carcass of the leopard in its hands. It rises to its full height, twice that of the ape, and raises the trophy high with its muscular arm. It lets out a long, guttural cry. He is a man, carnal and primeval; he is Tarzan of the Jungle.

Tarzan is the story of a wild feral child who is raised by great apes in the East African jungle. He was adopted by the colony as a baby after his explorer parents were marooned and killed. Since Edgar Rice Burrows created the fiction in 1912, this jungle man has become one of the most famous literary characters in the world, and the tale has been adapted into innumerable adventures.

The very first Tarzan movie was a black and white silent film made in 1918. Since then, scores of Tarzan movies have entertained audiences right up to the present day. Tarzan has also appeared in countless books, comic strips and in radio and television serials. The immediate appeal is obvious: the sensational excitement of man versus beast. Bare handed fights with wild animals, death defying leaps from waterfalls - what's not to like?

But behind the action, Tarzan is also a tale about nature and nurture. It's a story that explores psychological and social themes of environment and identity, as well as 'the survival of the fittest'. We're fascinated by the way the child is raised by the great apes because he grows up walking like an ape, talking like an ape and often looking like one too. The boy is brought up in an ape world, and sees and thinks like an ape. But we, the audience, know that he is not an ape; he is one of us.

Tarzan is a wild man, primitive and carnal, unaware of the outside world. He has never encountered another of his kind until one day a group of European explorers stumble upon him. Among them is an English woman, Jane Porter, who quickly realises that despite his wild form and behaviour, he is not an animal but a human being. And even more than that, he must be the lost and assumed dead, John Clayton, Viscount Greystoke. He is the sole inheritor of his esteemed father's estate.

A new nature

The revelation is staggering. Imagine a grand country Estate in England, such as Downton Abbey, or Mr Darcy's Pemberley in Pride and Prejudice – what a contrast between the jungle life of Tarzan and the vast inheritance of Viscount Greystoke. Tarzan lives by tooth and claw and the law of the jungle, but Viscount Greystoke is a man of wealth and high social standing amongst men. Let's say, for example, that like the great stately home of Downton, Greystoke Hall is a classic Georgian manor with 60-80 bedrooms sitting in a 5,000 acre estate of farmland with a veritable army of house servants and labourers. Perhaps his Estate, like Mr Darcy's, affords John Clayton a handsome income of £10,000 annually; that's about a million dollars a year in today's money.

This contrast between the 'survival of the fittest' jungle life and that of privileged inheritance is a useful analogy of our situation when we are born again by the Spirit of God. The Apostle Paul writes that we have been changed in our very nature. We are no longer carnal or animal-like, but divine in nature; we are a new creation (2 Corinthians 5:17).

Without the redeeming work of God we are basically selfish and insecure, living our lives in a dog-eat-dog world. However, this old nature is transformed when we receive the Holy Spirit and this changes our very identity. The Bible teaches that by God's grace we become divine aristocracy: **"a chosen people, a royal priesthood, a holy nation"** (1 Peter 2:9). Paul was so utterly convinced of this change in nature that he even rebuked one of the early churches for behaving like 'mere humans' (1 Corinthians 3:3).

In the story of Tarzan, when Jane Porter discovers the muscular John Clayton swinging from tree to tree, she realises that despite his appearance, he is in fact a very rich man of fortune and consequence, (as it turns out, it's a winning combination as far as

Jane's concerned!). However, when Tarzan is first discovered, in his thinking and self-identity he is an animal, living in an animal world. He even has an animal name. But from that moment of revelation, courtesy of Jane, he has to begin wrapping his mind around his true identity. He has to begin living according to the name, nature and inheritance his father has given him.

Life changing inheritance

Can you imagine the challenge this must have been to his mind? The change in his reality is so staggering that at first he would barely have had the ability to understand what it even meant. For a start, he wouldn't even have the language to comprehend it, he would have needed to learn how to speak English. He is Viscount John Clayton by inheritance. He didn't deserve it or earn it, he was born into it. It's the kind of privilege that comes as a gift and it's a picture of what happens to us when we are born again by the Spirit of God:

"When you believed, you were marked in him with a seal, the promised Holy Spirit, who is a deposit guaranteeing our inheritance until the redemption of those who are God's possession—to the praise of his glory." Ephesians 1:13-14

The Amplified Bible brings out the full meaning of the word 'deposit': **"The Spirit is the guarantee [the first instalment, the pledge, a foretaste] of our inheritance."**

The Bible teaches that as believers our inheritance comes in two parts: the down payment or advance and the final settlement. The final settlement is our glorious destiny – the future resurrection of our bodies when Jesus makes all things new (1 Thessalonians 4:16). Traditionally, many have come to assign the greater part of this gift to the future, but I believe it's a mistake to assign the greater portion of our inheritance to some future event.

We have been given an advance that is not insubstantial. Why? Because this verse from Ephesians tells us that our deposit is *God Himself*. This changes everything for us, not in some distant future, but right here and right now. It means that we have the transforming and empowering presence of the Holy Spirit in our lives today. Could it be that the advance we receive is even more transformational than the final balance?

When Jesus described to his disciples this advance on our future inheritance, He told them, **"You will be clothed with power from on high"** (Luke 24:49). If this advance is meant to prepare us for future glory I want to suggest to you that it is a far greater portion than we dared to believe. After all, the purpose of the advance is that the beneficiary takes on more and more responsibility until he or she is operating in the fullness of inheritance in all but name.

Learning to live by the Spirit

Getting back to our Tarzan analogy, let's imagine him shaved, dressed and in his stately home of Greystoke Hall. Everything is new and mysterious to him because he is surrounded by technologies he has never known or experienced. When he first sees a camera or a telephone he thinks they are supernatural or miraculous. This is part of the entertainment of the story as we watch Tarzan jump at the ringtone, and then drop the phone in shock as he hears Jane's voice. He stares at the device in horror, "Jane, how did you get in there?" But he will learn how to use these technologies and they will become *normal life*. He no longer needs to rely on yodelling as loudly as he can to communicate over great distances; he can video call to the other side of the world.

In a similar way, when we are born of the Spirit, our spiritual senses come alive and this newfound dimension can at first be surprising, or even intimidating. However, this divinely empowered or supernatural life is now normal life and is meant to bring an end to our carnal insecurities.

When we're born again into this new identity given us by our Heavenly Father, we have a lot of learning and growing up to do. Just like John Clayton, we must put off our 'animal thinking' and learn the new ways of the Spirit (Romans 8). This is why Paul exhorts us in much of his writing to put off the old nature and put on the new (Colossians 3:5-10, Ephesians 4:22-24). We need to learn how to listen and speak in the new language of the Spirit and manage our spiritual estate (or inheritance).

> " *It's going to be a long and challenging adventure, often humbling, but also rewarding and deeply affirming* "

It's going to be a long and challenging adventure, often humbling, but also rewarding and deeply affirming. We will learn to become who we are born to be. It's our Heavenly Father's desire that the low state He has lifted us from will spur us on to live honourable and morally good lives, rather than squander our new-found wealth on mere 'animal living'. His desire is that we come to the full maturity of His son Jesus as we walk in true love and power, because that's the high calling available to us all.

The miraculous ministry of Jesus

Few people can be said to have lived a more extraordinary life than Jesus. His life on earth was characterised by a combination of incredible love and amazing spiritual power. When we look at the gospel accounts, we see that not only did Jesus perform a great deal of miracles, He also did a great variety of miracles. For example, there was walking on water, healing the lame, blind and lepers, feeding the five thousand and raising the dead. Though at first there may seem to be no apparent pattern to the miracles Jesus performed, they can be categorised into three main types:

- **Miracles of Provision**
  (eg: feeding the 5,000 and turning water into wine)

- **Miracles of Healing**
  (eg: healing of the man blind from birth)

- **Miracles of Authority**
  (eg: calming of the waves and walking on water)

Any miracles of Jesus that provided food or sustenance, such as the miraculous catch of fish, we may categorise as miracles of provision. Miracles of healing are obvious; they don't just include physical healing but spiritual restoration too, including reconciliation and forgiveness. And authority? In one sense, all miracles are an act of authority (Jesus *commands* the lame to walk), but this is specifically authority over spiritual powers. Jesus didn't only preach with authority but also demonstrated His authority over both spiritual and natural worlds. Therefore, in the natural realm He commanded a fig tree to shrivel up and die (which it duly did), He went for a walk on the Sea of Galilee, and a storm obeyed Him when He told it to be quiet. Jesus' spiritual authority was also manifestly demonstrated when He commanded evil spirits to stop tormenting people and they had to obey Him.

Jesus declared that He had not come to abolish the law and the prophets but to fulfil them (Matthew 5:17), so it should be no surprise that the miracles of Jesus relate to three major themes that run throughout the Scriptures. These themes are like a plaited cord that weaves its way from the beginning, throughout the ages and resolves like a Celtic pattern in the new heaven and the new earth at the end of all things.

This threefold cord links the three temptations of Eve in the Garden of Eden to the three temptations of Jesus in the wilderness. It flows through the Old Testament and into the New, winding its way through the church ages and the times we live in, the last

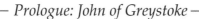

days. As we trace its course we find that there is nothing random or periphery about miracles; they are fundamental to the story, linking the very beginning with the very end. And what's more, we too have a part to play in God's threefold miracle mandate.

Chapter One:
Why Miracles?

"...the Father, abiding continually in Me, does His works [His attesting miracles and acts of power]... I assure you and most solemnly say to you, anyone who believes in Me [as Savior] will also do the things that I do; and he will do even greater things than these..." John 14:10-12 AMP

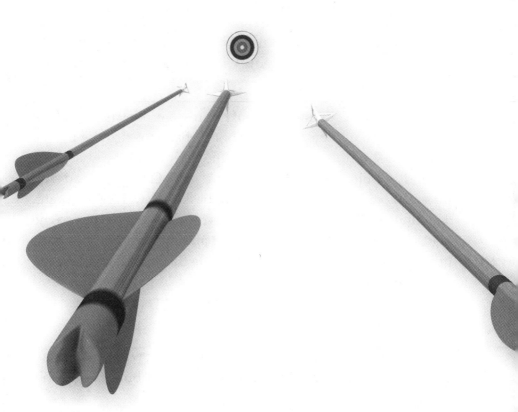

As our hot air balloon basket collided with the desert floor, we held on for our lives. I hadn't expected to be doing that on a cold morning in Arizona but there you are, or there we were; me and my wife Aliss in a crash landing. The billowing balloon relentlessly dragged us across the stony, cactus riddled landscape and there was nothing we could do about it but hold on and pray.

Aliss has always been good at selling. Give her a phone and a list of 'prospects' and she'd smash the targets every time. It was the mid 1990's and as one of the top achievers that year, her employer had treated us to a week of corporate rewards in Scottsdale, Arizona. That morning had meant an early start before sunrise and boarding buses in the dark. We were off to fly with other high achievers to enjoy balloon rides across the stunning desert plains.

I remember feeling nervous as they inflated the balloons in the cold dawn light because I'd never been great with heights, but I thought, 'Hey, these guys know what they're doing, what could possibly go wrong?'

The experience was surreal but impressive; the vastness of the crystal clear blue skies, the other hot air balloons drifting by, the intense heat of the gas burner on the back of my head and the ground slipping away beneath our feet. Our pilot had run through some safety spiel before our basket of twelve took flight. 'Landing position one,' he hollered, 'is to brace yourself like so': he held on tight to the basket sides. Landing position two is to hunker down and brace yourself inside the basket, and landing position three…' he paused here for effect, 'is to place your head between your knees and kiss yourself goodbye.' Everyone had a little laugh at that, but it wasn't funny anymore.

We'd begun to suspect there was something wrong when our pilot tried to bring the balloon down to land but changed his mind at the last minute. Unfortunately, despite routine weather checks the wind speed had picked up, the ground was moving too fast and we were in trouble. I feel the term 'pilot' here is a little generous for a hot air balloon operative because they have little scope for control; it's basically a choice of up or down. In our case we were running out of time and, like it or not, we had to land.

Our basket bumped and banged the earth a couple of times at speed and then tipped onto its side as our rogue balloon, reluctant to stop, began to drag us along. We were crouching inside, on our backs and holding on as tightly as possible. The less fortunate, including Aliss and I, were in the compartments directly in contact with the ground. We'd had a couple of days out in the desert already so we knew what that meant; big rocks, huge cacti the size of trees and other forbidding thorny hazards. We were frightened and giddy with adrenalin fuelled hysteria. Every time we felt ourselves hitting something big, the basket would jerk and everyone inside would yell and scream.

Navigating life's ups and downs

So, there we were getting dragged along when suddenly, 'Wham!' we hit something big and hard. We finally ground to a merciful halt and everyone breathed a sigh of relief as they climbed awkwardly, or were pulled out of the overturned basket. Grateful to be standing on solid ground we saw that a huge hole had been torn in the thick woven rattan, and it was right where Aliss had been. She seemed to have come off worst with a pain in her shoulder from the collision. Others were pulling cactus barbs out of their arms and shoulders. Undeterred, the balloon company encouraged everyone to perform the customary champagne and photo ceremony, but strangely, nobody seemed to be in the mood. Aliss and I eventually went off in an ambulance to get her shoulder checked out at a local hospital.

Many decisions in life can put us in situations we never planned or wanted to be in. We climb aboard some promising prospect, and though we do our best to navigate the ups and downs, ultimately there are things outside of our control that are hard to predict. If you're a member of humanity then welcome to adversity; not one of us is immune from it. Incomes can dry up, sickness can strike without warning and wicked, unscrupulous people can inflict all kinds of cruelties upon the innocent.

Though this is a universal truth, I also believe there are reasons why 'bad things happen' and we don't have to be helpless victims of these troubles. This doesn't mean that bad things will never happen to us, but it does mean we can live a life free from the tyranny of adversity. It means we can have a faith that changes circumstances through the supernatural power of God, a love that overcomes and a sure hope for a better future.

God believes in atheists

In her book, 'A Diary of Miracles Part II', Aliss shares many stories about everyday people who were surprised by God in our gift shop. I was often there as the healing miracles happened.

One Monday it was a Bank holiday, so our staff and volunteers had a day off. However, we wondered if it might be busy in town so we went in and opened up the shop. Usually Aliss would look after business at the front ('Hello, how can I help you?') and I'd serve coffee at the back ('Two cappuccinos and a slice of cake please.'). If customers came in, Aliss would often tell them about the miracles we'd seen and offer prayer for healing.

That day it was a musician from Liverpool who was visiting Chester with his wife who came into the shop. He told us that a musical for which he'd written the score was being aired that weekend on the radio. He was limping so Aliss asked him what the trouble was. The man described how he'd suffered from sciatica for years, the sciatic nerve in his leg was trapped and it caused him a lot of pain. The doctors were unable to remedy it.

Seizing the opportunity, Aliss enthusiastically told him about the power of Jesus. Not unkindly, the man explained he was an atheist and didn't believe in God at all, so there was no point. Undeterred, Aliss insisted that God believed in him all the same and convinced him to let her have a go. She told him, "If there isn't a God, nothing will happen. But if there is a God, then give Him a chance to prove Himself."

> " *It means we can have a faith that changes circumstances through the supernatural power of God* "

The man thought this wasn't unreasonable so he relented and let her pray. She asked him, "Were you in pain before I prayed?" He told her he had been in a lot of pain for some time. Then she asked him, "What's the pain like now?" and he admitted that he could feel no pain, even when he bent over and did squats. He said that was unusual and he looked very surprised. His wife, who was standing behind him, exclaimed, "See! I told you there was a God." The man was speechless.

How essential are miracles?

We feel honoured that God has given us the opportunity to see so many miraculous healings like this first hand. Not only that, but now we have the privilege of encouraging and training others to do the same. It's so tremendously rewarding to see a believer step out in faith for the first time and perform a miracle.

However, after all these years I've come to realise that if this spiritual activity is to be valued and sustainable, it's also important to know why we can do so and what our reasons are for pursuing the miraculous. Are they an 'optional extra' to the Christian faith? A kind of icing on the cake? Or is there something more substantial and vital to this dimension of the Holy Spirit lifestyle? After all, areas like healing ministry are a tough battleground, and if we are to overcome in this sphere we need to know more than just *how* to do it. We must have a sure confidence in *why* we are contending for miracles and *what* their real purpose is.

Chapter Two:
God's Threefold Blessing

"The LORD replied to them:
'I am sending you grain, new wine and olive oil,
enough to satisfy you fully.'" Joel 2:19

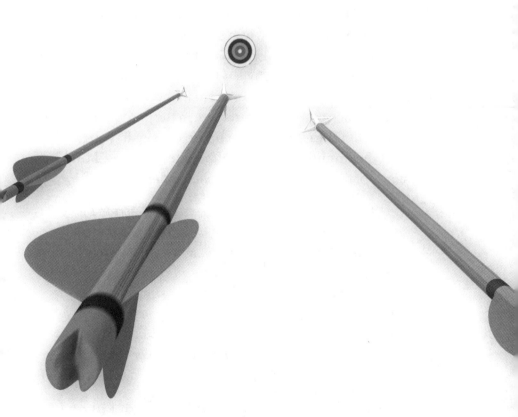

L ike all good theology we must start at the beginning. God created the heavens and the earth, and every living thing that grows; the fish, the birds of the air and all creatures great and small. He then planted a garden, a special place of habitation for His beloved mankind, in Eden:

"Now the LORD God had planted a garden in the east, in Eden; and there he put the man he had formed." Genesis 2:8

Genesis chapter two paints a wonderful picture of this paradise where the first people experienced harmony and wholeness. An abundance of fruitful trees grew in the garden and were 'good for food and pleasing to the eye'. The source of four rivers sprang up from the heart of Eden and watered the fertile land. God had placed the 'Tree of Life' in the garden, of which mankind was told to eat freely.

The 'Tree of the Knowledge of Good and Evil' was also in the garden but to eat of its fruit was strictly forbidden. These two trees represented freedom of choice between life in God and death outside of God, or between trust and fear. The man and woman were naked, open and innocent in their relationship with God and with each other. God put them in the garden to tend and enjoy it and Him forever. As I attempt to convey to you just how wonderful the original condition of humankind was, I find help in the words of the medieval mystic John Tauler[1]:

> *'It is impossible for us in words to describe the ineffable dignity of the soul, and we cannot in any way comprehend it. If we had here with us a human being in his primal nobility, pure as Adam in paradise in his natural state apart from grace, his simple nature unadorned - that person would be so luminous and pure, so ravishing and richly favoured by God that no one would be able to comprehend his purity nor with his reason conceive of it.'*

1. Johannes Tauler (1300 - 1361) - Sermon extract translated from the original German.

Suffice to say, a paradise world in which God abides and mankind is free and full of the joy of God's love is hard for us to imagine. Our greatest difficulty is that we view this world from the perspective of a fallen one and project a carnal understanding upon it. Yet the reality of Eden is deeply spiritual and was far more substantial or real than the transient life that we experience today.

> " *This seminal garden is a metaphor of Adam's life in God and the life we are called to live as believers* "

In many ways, this seminal garden is a metaphor of Adam's life in God and the life we are called to live as believers. It's a beautiful blueprint for God-centred living. The tree of life at the centre of the garden is a type of abiding in the divine or eternal life (John 6:53-58); rivers overflow from this centre just as the Holy Spirit flows from within us (John 7:38). The tree of the knowledge of good and evil in the garden represents the opportunity to make good choices every day by exercising faith and trust in God. The fruitfulness of the trees in the garden remind us of the fruit of the Spirit (Galatians 5:22-23), and the rich treasures in the lands that the rivers flow through, of the riches of God's grace (Ephesians 1:7). Adam's relationship with God also speaks of the unbroken and intimate fellowship we now have with our Heavenly Father through His son Jesus (John 17:21).

In Genesis chapter one we see the threefold blessing of God established for humankind. He blesses them with perfect provision, wholeness and authority:

PROVISION - God provides all they need for sustenance:

'Then God said, "I give you every seed-bearing plant on the face of the whole earth and every tree that has fruit with seed in it. They will be yours for food."' Genesis 1:29

WHOLENESS - God also imparts into their very nature His divine nature by breathing into them His own spirit or breath. This establishes a unique bond of love and unity as God makes them in His own image and commands them to increase in number:

'Then God said, "Let us make mankind in our image, in our likeness..."' Genesis 1:26

'God blessed them and said to them, "Be fruitful and increase in number."' Genesis 1:28

AUTHORITY - And God gives them delegated authority to rule over all other living creatures:

"...so that they may rule over the fish in the sea and the birds in the sky, over the livestock and all the wild animals, and over all the creatures that move along the ground." Genesis 1:26

In summary, the threefold blessing of God upon humanity is:

• **PROVISION** (which gives us security)

• **WHOLENESS** (which gives us love and acceptance)

• **AUTHORITY** (which gives us significance)

It's important that we engage our faith to believe that Eden is more than an unreachable ideal or a fantasy. This trinity of divine blessings is the eternal life that Jesus came to restore because it was lost. The book of Genesis tells the tragic story of how this cataclysmic event took place.

Paradise lost

We read in Genesis chapter three that the devil came to Eve in the form of a serpent and essentially did one thing; he planted a poisonous seed of doubt in her mind about God's goodness and His intentions towards them:

'Now the serpent was more crafty than any of the wild animals the Lord God had made. He said to the woman, "Did God really say, 'You must not eat from any tree in the garden'?"

The woman said to the serpent, "We may eat fruit from the trees in the garden, but God did say, 'You must not eat fruit from the tree that is in the middle of the garden, and you must not touch it, or you will die.'"

"You will not certainly die," the serpent said to the woman. "For God knows that when you eat from it your eyes will be opened, and you will be like God, knowing good and evil.'"

As the Scripture tells us, the devil is crafty, which means 'being clever at achieving one's aims by indirect or deceitful methods'. He does this effectively by mixing up truth and lies to create a convincing sounding falsehood. The fact is that his statement, **"For God knows that when you eat from it your eyes will be opened, and you will be like God, knowing good and evil"** is true. We know this because later in Genesis 3:22 we read: '**And the LORD God said, "The man has now become like one of us, knowing good and evil."'** However, combining this statement with the lie, **"You will not certainly die"**, creates a falsehood.

The only possible conclusion for Eve of this line of reasoning is that, 'God may be lying to me, and if He is lying to me, then He may be withholding something good from me'.

James 1:14-15 tells us that it's from the conceiving of the *desire* for the object of temptation (whatever that object may be) that sin is birthed. A process takes place inside the heart and mind of Adam and Eve before they commit the sin of eating the forbidden fruit. This conception of the first unfaithful desire is the root of all the other sins that follow it.

Writing in the fifth century, St. Augustine[2] explained in his Catechism that once we begin to consider it, there is pride,

2. Augustine of Hippo (354 - 430) - *Enchiridion (on Faith, Hope, and Love)*

unbelief, murder, theft and more in that one sinful act. Everything that happens in this Genesis account is fundamental to our understanding of all that is painful and lacking in our world.

The tap root of temptation

This primary temptation warns us that the next time you or I have a thought process that concludes 'God is not good' or 'God is withholding something from me for no good reason', we know exactly where it came from. At the time, we may think this is a reasonable or harmless consideration, but in fact it's the most awful and ancient temptation of all. I once knew a guy who, though professing Jesus as his saviour, just couldn't get past this one sticking point of God's goodness towards him. His mantra was that he just wasn't one of God's special people; he insisted that the fullness of God's goodness just wasn't meant for him. This is our enemy's number one goal, and perhaps his only goal; to convince us to believe this lie. It's this seed of doubt, which was entertained, germinated and grew into the following three temptations which bear false witness to the reality of God's good nature.

Genesis 3 verse 6: "When the woman saw that the fruit of the tree was good for food and pleasing to the eye, and also desirable for gaining wisdom, she took some and ate it."

The seed of doubt sown by the devil fell on the soil of mankind's desire and germinated into a temptation with three distinct parts. The number three in Scripture often signifies 'completeness' and so we know they all grow from the same root; they are all manifestations of the same doubt. Eve saw that the fruit of the tree of the knowledge of good and evil was:

- GOOD FOR FOOD

- PLEASING TO THE EYE

- DESIRABLE FOR GAINING KNOWLEDGE

This trinity of temptations may remind readers of another Scripture in the New Testament. In his letter to believers, the Apostle John exhorts us to be separate from 'the world', meaning 'the fallen nature' of man:

"For everything in the world—the lust of the flesh, the lust of the eyes, and the pride of life—comes not from the Father but from the world." 1 John 2:16

These three worldly desires reflect the three seminal temptations in Genesis chapter 3:

- **THE DESIRE OF THE FLESH** (good for food)

- **THE LUST OF THE EYES** (pleasing to the eye)

- and **THE PRIDE OF CARNAL LIFE**
  (desirable for gaining knowledge)

This threefold root of sinful desire springs from the tap root of doubt and mistrust of God's goodness towards us. Each of these temptations, when acted upon, had catastrophic consequences for Adam and Eve and subsequently for us and our world. We will explore the nature of those consequences or curses more fully in the coming chapters, but they are summarised here in a table.

This simple table shows the sin manifested in each temptation and its corresponding curse:

Temptation at the fall:	Sin committed when temptation acted upon:	Curse released by the sin:
Good for food	Doubt in God's provision for me	Famine (a lack of provision)
Pleasing to the eye	Doubt in God's love of me	Disease (a lack of health or wholeness)
Desirable for gaining knowledge	Doubt in God's authority over me	War (a lack of peace)

Because God's *provision* for us is complete, the only place we can go in our mistrust of that provision is into a state of lack. Because God's *love* for us is complete, when we doubt that love we can only experience separation and a lack of wholeness. If we desire *knowledge* beyond a complete submission to God in our relationship with him, we submit ourselves to the power of God's enemies, which results in conflict and slavery. These curses are the result of sin and they culminate in the ultimate curse of death. Therefore, God said to mankind:

"He must not be allowed to reach out his hand and take also from the tree of life and eat, and live forever." Genesis 3:22

What we will now explore is how each of these areas of disobedience manifests throughout the Biblical account and how Jesus' mission to **'seek and to save that which was lost'** (Luke 19:10) deals so victoriously and absolutely with each one.

The serpent came to steal, kill and destroy, and through sin the curse of death was released upon mankind. Jesus came to reverse this curse and restore us to 'life in all its fulness'; resurrection life, even eternal life (John 10:10,28). We will see how this threefold restoration of blessing was established in the life of Jesus and demonstrated through the miracles He performed. And furthermore, how through the transforming power of the cross He empowers us to do the same; to receive God's blessings and release His power.

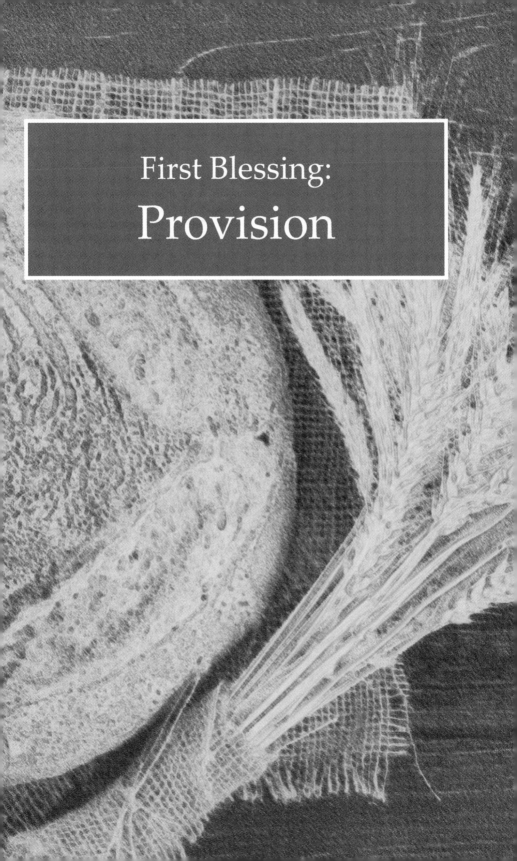

First Blessing:
Provision

Chapter Three:
The Source of Lack

"Which of you, if your son asks for bread,
will give him a stone?" Matthew 7:9

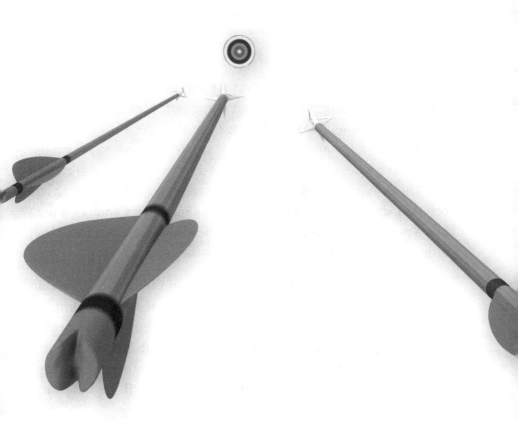

I have a vivid memory of jogging down a cold, wet country road one Autumn morning and pleading with God, "Please deliver me and my family from this crushing debt." It was a season in my life when I went for a run on most mornings. I would set out very early and run about four miles down through the village. There was a disused railway line that had been covered with asphalt and converted into a cycle path. I headed out over the fields and away from the traffic. I liked the solitude of day break, the misty air and the birdsong of the dawn chorus.

Aliss and I had renovated a village cottage and coach house dating back to 1740 and made it into a beautiful family home. It had old low beams, open fireplaces and a Tudor style black and white fascia. With a lot of help from Aliss' dad David, we had increased the value of our property, but it meant we had been tempted to use the equity to fund our struggling business. We unwisely re-mortgaged our house several times to free up the cash we needed to keep it all going. At the time it felt like we didn't have much choice.

This resulted in us having an alarmingly high personal debt with a massive monthly payment going out. This was bad with a capital 'B'. This is the kind of situation that destroys marriages, breaks up families and makes people sick with stress, so as I jogged along the bridle path I cried out to God for help; what else could I do? The outlook was bleak. At best we were heading for losing our beloved 'dream home', being left with a huge debt and no way to buy a new one, and at worst we were heading for bankruptcy. I felt vulnerable and alone, the situation was desperate.

I reach out now to that young man jogging through the rain and tell him it's going to be alright. I tell him to hold on tight, it's going to be a bumpy ride, but it's going to be better than alright; it's going to be nothing short of miraculous. Within three years we had no debt, we owned our own house outright and perhaps what is even more amazing, our family was still together and

Aliss and I were enjoying married life more than ever. There was no 'quick fix' of winning the lottery or a 'business angel' bail out. We gave up our dream home, the business and everything that went with it. We didn't realise how much of a burden it had become until we moved into our new, relatively modest, mortgage-free home. We instantly felt the release and peace of freedom. It was priceless.

The temptation of 'the desire of the flesh'

The devil came to the Garden of Eden to undermine the 'God-centredness' of Adam and Eve. As a fallen angel, the devil had been cast down from heaven as punishment for his pride, because he said, **"I will make myself like the Most High"** (Isaiah 14:12-14). The devil had possessed or co-habited the physical body of an animal called a serpent or dragon and the spirit and the animal are spoken of as if they are one. The Scriptures (in various places) refer to the serpent both as an animal and as the spirit we know as the devil.

Often when there is a spirit power behind a physical body, Scripture will speak of them interchangeably. This helps us understand how Genesis recounts God cursing both an animal called a serpent ("Cursed are you above all livestock and all wild animals!" Genesis 3:14), and the devil ("I will put enmity between you and the woman" Genesis 3:15), all at once. The spiritual and physical are intertwined. If the devil/serpent could only convince the human creatures that God was withholding something good from them, something that they lacked and needed, then death would surely follow. But how could he do that when they already had everything?

What was God withholding?

Now to be clear, God was evidently withholding something from mankind because He had forbidden the eating of it.

However, what God had forbidden was not something mankind needed in any way, shape or form. Every parent knows that to care for and protect their child they must withhold things that would harm them. A good parent gives their all for their child, they hold nothing back of themselves (and as Jesus pointed out to us, God is a far better parent than any earthly one, Luke 11:13). The truth is, all that God was withholding from the first people was a terrible existence outside of His perfect provision for body, spirit and soul. In other words, God was withholding 'lack', not provision.

Eve saw that it was good for food

Tragically, Eve began to entertain this diabolical 'withholding something good' suggestion when she came to her first conclusion about the forbidden fruit, that it was **'good for food'**. The irony of this thought is that Adam and Eve were surrounded by a garden of physically and spiritually sustaining food (including the tree of life), and there was simply no need there to satisfy. The thought or temptation was an illusion or **"a vain imagining setting itself up against the knowledge of God"** (2 Corinthians 10:5).

This is an *imagining* we can still fall for today. The devil's strategy is always 'smoke and mirrors'. Rarely will he directly challenge our trust in God. He prefers to simply persuade us to entertain the idea that God does not want, or is not able, to provide all we need. If he can persuade us to look for provision in anything that is outside of God's perfect provision then his job is done. Entertaining a thought such as this is like looking for sustenance in a pile of dung. Believe me, there just isn't anything good to eat in there.

The result of disobedience

Everything that God gave mankind authority over, both spiritual and physical, was influenced by their behaviour (and still is). Therefore, the choice of Adam and Eve to disobediently look outside of God's perfect provision manifested in the physical world around them as the dreadful curse of lack and poverty. Because Adam and Eve had chosen lack, that is what they released and received in their sphere of influence. Every type of famine and ruined harvest ever to have blighted the world has come from this one root. Though we are quick to call them 'acts of God' they are the result of 'acts of men'. We may think that the curses

> " *Sometimes we have to let go of the very thing we thought was God's gift to us in order to have the real treasure* "

God declared over Adam and Eve in Genesis 3 were random punishments made up on a whim, but this is not true. God simply told Adam and Eve what the consequence of their disobedience was:

"Cursed is the ground because of you; through painful toil you will eat food from it all the days of your life. It will produce thorns and thistles for you, and you will eat the plants of the field." Genesis 3:17-18

Is it possible to sow lack in our lives? Of course it is. Whenever we are greedy or selfish or withholding, we sow seeds all around us of mistrust in God's provision for us. It's hard when you're in a situation like we were with our failing business. It can feel like there is no way out. However, we had to learn, perhaps the hard way, that sometimes we have to let go of the very thing we thought was God's gift to us in order to have the real treasure. We had to make a lot of difficult decisions but the most important one was humbling ourselves and listening hard to the Holy Spirit. For a while we thought this meant getting friends over and praying for the business to succeed, but ultimately God had better plans.

When 'provision' is not a blessing

I read in the news recently that the 'new malnutrition' is obesity. On the face of it that sounds like a mistake. Surely the great problem facing the world today in terms of nourishment is lack of food – the starving millions? But no, BBC news reported that: *'The 2016 Global Nutrition Report said 44% of countries were now experiencing "very serious levels" of both under-nutrition and obesity.'*

Apparently, being malnourished through eating the wrong thing is the new normal; it's happening in nearly every country and causing a global epidemic of high cholesterol and diabetes. The report demands that governments begin to understand that malnourishment doesn't just mean not getting enough food but it also means getting the *wrong* food.

This is a modern phenomenon of a society 'blessed' with an abundance of provision. The average person in the west today has a variety of international food available to them that, in the not too distant past, kings would only have dreamt of. And yet we are unable to find satisfaction. The food we are eating doesn't actually feed us, it makes us unwell. This is surely symptomatic of an underlying spiritual malnutrition: an inability to find satisfaction in God.

God's provision is relational

When God provides, He doesn't just give us 'things', He builds into His provision a relationship with Himself. Our testimony is that the Holy Spirit will guide you step by step if you allow Him to. Miracles of fulfilling provision come through humility, trust and obedience. After we closed our business, Aliss started a joint venture which brought us enough income to stay in our dream home and pay our huge monthly bills. We initially thought this was the answer but it was just the beginning. The Holy Spirit subsequently told us to do things that didn't make sense at the time; to give up this career and lucrative income and to start an outreach programme in a nearby needy neighbourhood. He told us not to sell the house yet but to hold on, even though we had virtually no income. How were we to know that the value of houses would rocket that year? Eleven months later the Lord then told us to sell our dream home, and when we did, we had enough money to buy a lovely house in the same village and be mortgage free.

You might say we got lucky, but it was more than that, because God changed us in our hearts and attitudes too. We even realised that the Lord had provided financially for the four of us (Aliss and I and our two children, 8 and 12 years old at the time) to go to ministry school in America for a whole year. I am convinced we would not have chosen that path if we had not been through that test. We have lived our lives very differently ever since. The ministry school experience helped birth works of God in our lives that went beyond our wildest dreams and have subsequently impacted thousands. God's ways are not our ways and they don't often make sense, but our testimony is that He is the best at providing what we *really* need.

Israel and the blessing of provision

The Old Testament is bursting with accounts of God's supernatural interventions with people. From Moses and the burning bush to Elisha and the jars of oil, each and every story seems to be accompanied by miraculous events. Many times, these stories illustrate how God's intention is to restore a people of faith and trust to come back into His care and provision.

In the book of Exodus we read how God raised up Moses to help deliver the Israelite slaves from Egypt. This was accompanied by many miraculous signs culminating in the epic parting of the Red Sea which allowed the Israelites to escape their captivity. One of the first trials or tests for them as they wandered in the wilderness was that of physical hunger. It brought them to the brink of starvation and they began to fail. They complained to Moses that back in Egypt they'd had all the food they needed, but in the desert there was no food at all; their fresh food was long gone. That's a lot of hungry people with very little to look forward to. However, much like Dorothy in The Wizard of Oz who exclaimed, 'We're not in Kansas anymore', they had to learn that all the rules of 'normal life' had changed. They were now the people of the God of miracles. A lesson we are still learning today.

It's in this account where we discover the very first mention in the Biblical narrative of God's glory, and it's linked with supernatural provision. Moses told the people: **"In the morning you will see the glory of the Lord"** (Exodus 16:7). God did an amazing thing for this whole multitude of migrating slaves. He demonstrated His glory to the Israelites by providing manna: miraculous bread from heaven which appeared on the ground, fresh every morning.

One of the major themes of the liberation of Israel in the book of Exodus is that of personal transformation. In order to remove the self-identity of lack and poverty from their thinking, God had to break off their utter identification with that slave mentality. It's a picture of how God wants to reverse the curse of lack by restoring His place in our lives as our sole provider.

This manna or food from God seemed to have similar qualities to grain because the Israelites made it into cakes and it tasted like honey. One characteristic of this Heavenly bread was that it had to be eaten on the same day it arrived. It was daily bread. The Israelites who tried to store it against God's instructions soon found that their stash of saved food was full of maggots and corruption. Surely this speaks of the source of heavenly provision in our own lives being in our daily relationship with God. He wants to speak to you and through you today; that's your soul food. In Matthew's gospel Jesus taught us to pray, '**Give us *this*** *day* **our daily bread'**, not yesterday's or tomorrow's bread of life, but life in all its fullness today.

In the table below I've added a fourth development to the story of divine provision. The first columns show how the temptation and the subsequent sin lost divine provision and released lack. The last column shows how God begins to restore this blessing back to His people Israel.

Temptation at the fall:	Sin committed when temptation acted upon:	Curse released by the sin:	Blessing to Israel:
Good for food	Doubt in God's provision for me	Famine (a lack of provision)	Manna in the wilderness

Chapter Four:
Restoration of Provision

"Give me neither poverty nor riches, but give me only my daily bread." Proverbs 30:8

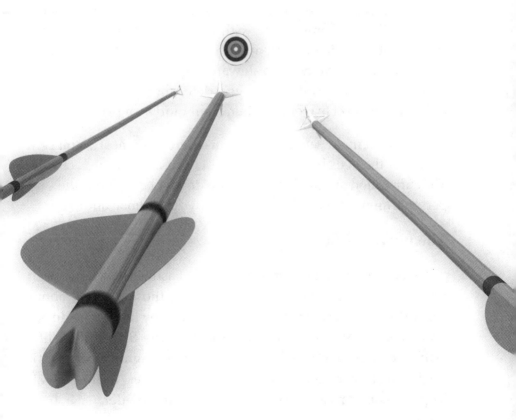

Around 1,500 years after the Israelites had entered the Sinai desert, the Israelite man Yeshua (יֵשׁוּעַ - the Hebrew name from which we derive the name Jesus) was led into the wilderness by the Holy Spirit.

"Jesus, full of the Holy Spirit, left the Jordan and was led by the Spirit into the wilderness." Luke 4:1

After His baptism, Jesus went alone into the desert and fasted for 40 days. The parallel here between Jesus and the Israelites' 'baptism' through the Red Sea and subsequent 40 years of testing in the wilderness is striking. Jesus said He had not come to abolish the law and the prophets but to fulfil them. Where others had tried and failed, the Messiah would succeed.

One of the chief characteristics of Jesus' 'temptation in the wilderness' is that it was a time of solitude. He was alone for a long time and yet we know He would not have been lonely because He was communing with His Heavenly Father. This is significant for us in our preparation for and desire to move in the miraculous. Our capacity to steward the true power of the Holy Spirit in any public setting is largely determined by how we learn obedience to our Heavenly Father in our hidden or private life.

The wilderness sets the stage for one of the most significant battles of the ages between the Son of Man and our arch enemy. The temptation of Jesus is an epic showdown played out in the very personal arena of solitude; there is no physical human audience.

The power of fasting

Jesus was also fasting from food. Fasting has long been recognised as a powerful discipline by those serious about cultivating a God centred life. Often derided by those who do not understand the role of self-discipline in the Spirit filled life, fasting can be a powerful tool if handled rightly, because it teaches us how to control our physical appetites. In this way, it helps us to affirm God as our sole source and provider.

Ironically the danger of any self-discipline is that if handled wrongly it can make us even more self-centred. (The Apostle Paul is keen to point this out in Colossians 2:23). However, when undertaken with humility and reverence for God, the corresponding freedom that physical fasting brings is that of a deeper satisfaction in God. The fourth century theologian Athenasius wrote:

"Fasting possesses great power and it works glorious things. To fast is to banquet with angels."[1]

Fasting is a useful tool that assists us into the spiritual maturity of being joyful in God regardless of external physical discomforts.

Temptation and testing

Temptation and testing are not the same thing. James 1:13 says, **'When tempted, no one should say, "God is tempting me." For God cannot be tempted by evil, nor does he tempt anyone'**. Temptation is a malicious act because its goal is to bring its victim into a place of failure and condemnation. Temptations are designed to ensnare, to entrap and even to enslave, and they are altogether the work of our adversary.

God does not tempt us, but He does test us. The testings of God are far more magnanimous than temptation because His aim is to bring us into a place of victory and maturity. Rick Joyner (MorningStar Ministries) puts it like this, 'We do not fail God's tests, we just keep on taking them until we pass them.' However, when Jesus was led into the wilderness to be tempted by the devil it was to fight a deadly battle; the enemy wanted Jesus to fail and fall in defeat.

The battlefield

When we compare the temptation of Jesus to that of Adam and Eve in Genesis 3, the arenas for their respective temptations are

1. Athanasius of Alexandria (298 - 373)

poles apart. In His time of testing, Jesus was not in a paradise garden surrounded by fruit trees, He was in a wilderness completely devoid of provision. Not only was there no food to be found but Jesus had fasted for 40 days. This is the utter limit of a food fast before the physical body begins to be damaged, so Jesus had every reason to be physically hungry. The

> " *In reality the aggressor was Jesus and the devil was simply defending his home ground* "

Scripture categorically tells us, **'He was hungry'** (Luke 4:2), because it's important for us to know that Jesus in his humanity experienced physical hunger just as we do. It was in this environment of barrenness and lack that the devil came to try his hand once again to subdue God's beloved.

Dominion and authority

Unlike Adam, Jesus was born into a world where the devil had already established dominion and power. The prophet Isaiah described it as **'thick darkness covering the earth'** (Isaiah 60:2) and the Apostle Paul called it **'the dominion of darkness'** (Colossians 1:13). Dominion refers to authority and power over *domains* and Jesus as the Son of Man entered this arena to fight for those territories and take them back for mankind. A superficial reading of this passage may give us the impression that the devil was the one attacking Jesus, but in reality the aggressor was Jesus and the devil was simply defending his home ground. In any earthly fight for territorial dominion, a nation will always unleash its military power whenever its territory is threatened by an outside force. The spiritual world is no different and the demonic realm will tend to manifest aggressively when there is a threat to its occupancy.

This is why, during the deliverance of individual people from demonic oppression, evil spirits will often show themselves by belligerent behaviour such as *'loud shrieks'* (Acts 8:7). We should not be intimidated if this happens, but rather encouraged, because it means the enemy is alarmed. When Jesus entered the final stages of his testing in the wilderness, the devil was forced into a confrontation with Him. Though the Holy Spirit had led Jesus into the wilderness, it was not as a victim, but as a dread champion.

The gospel accounts of Jesus' temptation in the wilderness (found in Matthew 4, Luke 4 and Mark 1) are the only times in the Gospels that the devil is said to talk to Jesus 'face to face'. The devil evidently knew that at this pivotal time of Christ's life, his rule and reign over the earth was about to be under serious threat from this Son of Man. The fact that Jesus, at His recent baptism, had had His identity as God's representative publicly declared in heaven and on earth must have confirmed a few things to His adversary. The fight that played out in the desert between Jesus and the devil was key to the messianic mission. Just as in the Garden of Eden, the suggestions of the serpent manifested in a trinity of temptations, so in the wilderness the devil used the same threefold tactic.

The first temptation: The arena of provision

The devil's first onslaught was to start with the most obvious temptation for one who is on the brink of starvation after a 40 day fast:

The devil came to him and said, "If you are the Son of God, tell these stones to become bread." Matthew 4:3

Behind this suggestion, we can hear the sibilant echo of the serpent in the Garden of Eden sowing seeds of doubt in God's goodness. However, despite His physical hunger, Jesus refused to question His own identity or entertain the thought that His life and provision could possibly come from any source other than His Heavenly Father:

Jesus answered, "It is written: 'Man shall not live on bread alone, but on every word that comes from the mouth of God.'" Matthew 4:4

Jesus confessed by faith that He was never going to elevate His physical needs above His trust in God. Looking more closely, we see that the real sting in the tail here is the devil's subtle, *'If you are the Son of God'* left hook. We can imagine, when he tempted Adam and Eve in the garden, that this was implied there too: 'Who do you think you are? Are you even allowed to think for yourselves? Are you really God's beloved children?' Jesus' response to this temptation was to reply with a quote from Scripture. It was from a passage in Deuteronomy which referred to the heavenly manna we looked at earlier:

"He humbled you, causing you to hunger and then feeding you with manna, which neither you nor your ancestors had known, to teach you that man does not live on bread alone but on every word that comes from the mouth of the Lord." Deuteronomy 8:3

This Scripture does not say that man does not need physical bread. God cares about our physical bodies. What it does say is that it's not primarily satisfying this need which ultimately sustains us. God responds to faith rather than need (see Hebrews 11:6). Later on in His teachings, Jesus used the symbolism of the bread and the stone in a parable to illustrate God's goodness by saying:

"Which of you, if your son asks for bread, will give him a stone?" Matthew 7:9

In other words, if you think you know how to be good parents then surely you understand that your perfect Heavenly Father is going to provide for you. We must settle it in our hearts that it is

God who ultimately sustains our lives. The temptation of Adam and Eve took place in a paradise of provisional blessing but their failure to trust God gave birth to a wilderness. The temptation of Jesus took place in the wilderness and his victory released streams of water that would restore paradise.

Temptation at the fall:	Sin committed when temptation acted upon:	Curse released by the sin:	Jesus' Temptation in the wilderness:
Good for food	Doubt in God's provision for me	Famine (a lack of provision)	Turn these stones into bread

Chapter Five:
Living from Abundance

"Come, all you who are thirsty, come to the
waters; and you who have no money,
come, buy and eat!" Isaiah 55:1

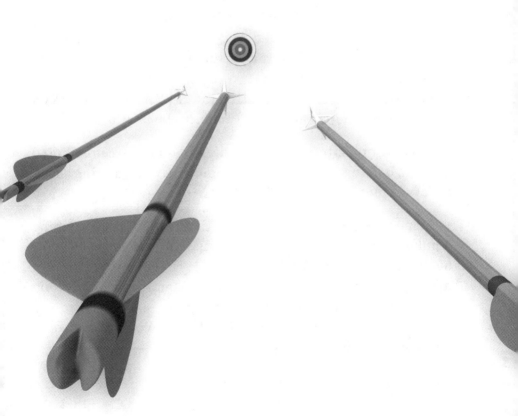

L iving in a paradigm of lack is not primarily about how much material wealth we have or do not have, but rather, it's about defining our lives by what limits us. To use an old analogy, it's perceiving the glass (no matter how big it may be), as being half empty instead of half full. It is not merely having a negative outlook, although it may include this, but it's a view of life that allows the fear of lack to dictate our choices.

Inevitably, this leads us to measure out everything we do with an imaginary pair of scales. It can cause us to become miserly or withholding with our time, our love and our material generosity. A paradigm of lack can even make us resentful and critical of the kindness of others because we become cynical about their motives.

The antidote to living under the curse of a poverty paradigm like this, is to immerse ourselves in the Word of God. This is because The Bible is the living Word of God (see Hebrews 4:12) and it has inherent power to break the spiritual chains of poverty in our lives. The Word is like seed that contains life and truth. These seeds of life will germinate and grow into overflow and abundance if we allow them to take root in the soil of our lives (see Matthew 13:1-23 'The parable of the sower'). There is no quick fix for those who desire real spiritual maturity, but for those who...

"...chew on Scripture day and night. You're a tree replanted in Eden, bearing fresh fruit every month, never dropping a leaf, always in blossom." Psalm 1:2-3 MSG

Remember I told you about the time I used to go running regularly? What I didn't mention was that I used to 'chew' or meditate on passages of the Bible as I jogged along. A friend of mine had told me he was in the habit of memorising and reciting whole passages, even chapters of Scripture, and it stoked my curiosity. How was that possible, and what would it be like to know Scripture in that way?

One bite at a time

There's an old saying that poses a big problem and gives wisdom in the answer: 'How do you eat an elephant? One bite at a time!' So, I started with Colossians and memorised the first line: **"Paul an Apostle of Christ Jesus by the will**

> " *The Word is like seed that contains life and truth* "

of God, and Timothy our brother". I read it before I set out and said it repeatedly when I went for my run. Later in the day I remembered it and checked back to make sure I was still saying it right. The next day I added the next line: **"To God's holy people in Colossae, the faithful brothers and sisters in Christ"** and did the same thing. To my delight and surprise, over the next weeks and months, in this way I gradually memorised the whole of Colossians 1, (a powerful Scripture containing the passage about the supremacy of Christ: **"The Son is the image of the invisible God"**). I would recite it in the car, whilst mowing the lawn and when I went to sleep at night.

Over time, God did a work in my heart and there began to be a shift in my thinking towards a Kingdom or heavenly paradigm. Life looked richer and filled with possibilities because I began to see the supremacy and sufficiency of Jesus in everything I did. Over the years I went on to memorise many more chapters, and in this way I would meditate on the Word day and night. Meditating on Scripture like this is the best remedy I know for breaking off a poverty spirit and allowing God to remove the limitations from our thinking. The language of Scripture is expansive and universal and it firmly seats us with Christ in heavenly places (Ephesians 2:6).

Eat the Word

In the Eucharist or The Lord's Supper the bread we share is a powerful symbol of the Lord's body broken for us. It's through the cross that we are set free from the curse of lack and brought into the freedom and blessing of provision. The bread is particularly symbolic of this aspect of the threefold blessing because it's made from wheat and is nourishing to our bodies. When you break bread with others, thank the Lord for His wonderful sacrifice and for the blessing of abundant provision that comes from eating the Bread of Life.

The Bible is intrinsically prophetic in nature because in its entirety it reveals the will of God. If we are to heed the exhortation of the Apostle Paul to **"Follow the way of love and eagerly desire gifts of the Spirit, especially prophecy"** (1 Corinthians 14:1), then having the discipline to meditate on Scripture is essential for anyone who would pursue it.

When we prophesy it's as if we are imparting spiritual bread into the lives of others. Becoming immersed in the living Word of God and getting the Word of God into us is the surest foundation for cultivating a prophetic lifestyle. If you set your heart on this one thing, it will make you an overflowing blessing to your family, church and friends. The good news is that all you need in order to accomplish this is a Bible. However, you will also need determination and creativity to effectively weave Bible meditation into your lifestyle. But if you do this, it will release the provision and love of God into your life to such an extent that it will overflow to others.

Second Blessing:
Wholeness

Chapter Six:
The Lust of the Eye

"Death and Destruction are never satisfied, and
neither are human eyes." Proverbs 27:20

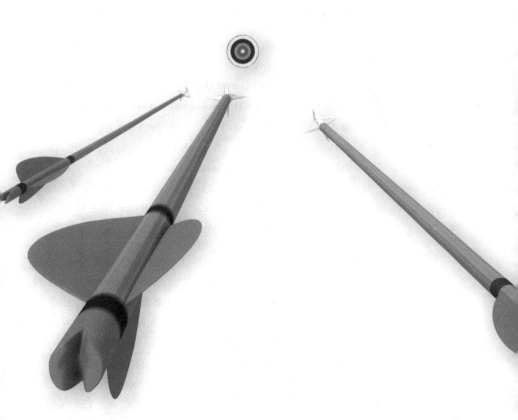

Some years ago, in my mid-thirties, I woke up to find my legs had become unbearably itchy and were beginning to turn quite purple (not a pleasant sight I can assure you)! After a couple of sleepless nights, I went to my doctor. She seemed quite pleased with the condition and told me that it 'beat treating people for coughs and colds'. She prescribed me some ointment to relieve the unbearable irritation and said she had to go away and find out more.

On my second visit, she gave the condition a serious sounding Latin name and told me that it was something to do with bone marrow and platelets in the blood causing bruising. She didn't know what had triggered it, but said it could be quite serious and was likely to affect me for the rest of my life. I searched for it on the internet and then wished I hadn't. I considered myself fairly fit and healthy and dealing with this kind of news was a new experience, so I shrugged it off and got on with life, as you do.

I vividly remember one day we were doing our weekly food shop in a local supermarket. There I was, minding my own business, when all of a sudden, I started to feel unaccountably emotional. It was one of those times when the routine of life is going on all around you and suddenly you feel an inexplicable tightness in your throat and an urge to sob. I wasn't sure what had come over me, but I think it was basically self-pity. I just about kept myself together, but I felt vulnerable and alone. Sickness, especially the prospect of long term sickness, can be like that. It's such a personal burden to come to terms with.

This was years before Aliss and I began to experience the kind of healing miracles we see today. However, we prayed in faith that night, we rebuked the diagnosis, and the condition quickly cleared up. And I am pleased to report that it has never happened again since. When I went back to the doctor she was surprised. I explained to her that we'd prayed for it to go and it had simply cleared up on its own. She agreed that faith was a very important and powerful thing.

It was that experience of unexpected emotion that had caught me off guard. The sudden feeling of sadness, like I was on my own, like I'd been abandoned. I think that's part of what sickness does; it makes us feel unloved and vulnerable. However, Scripture tells us that sickness and disease played no part in God's original creation. It was never meant to plague the lives of humankind and rob us of hope and life.

The completeness of God's love

As we reflect again on the good beginnings of humanity in the first chapters of Genesis, we are presented with a world of completeness and harmony. When God was speaking creation into existence we read that He repeatedly 'saw that it was good'; a divine perception and response that culminated with: **'on the sixth day he saw all that he had made was *very good*'** (Genesis 1:31 – italics added). This strongly expresses God's pleasure as He sees and enjoys His work of creation.

When God made mankind 'male and female' they were created in His own image:

**"So God created mankind in his own image,
in the image of God he created them;
male and female he created them." Genesis 1:27**

Because God is Spirit we know that it was the breathing of His Spirit into the dust of the ground that made mankind uniquely godlike in the created order. Though mankind is 'flesh and blood' they were given an immortality that blended flesh and spirit together. I don't believe that this first physical body was subject to the same rigours of corruption we know today. Bones did not wear out and organs did not deteriorate (or if they did, they regenerated continually).

Though we are told very little in Scripture about the nature of this original physical body, I want to suggest that we may take some clues from the resurrected body of Jesus. This is because we know that in His resurrected body, Jesus was not subject to physical death either. We are told He appeared in different and often unrecognised forms, and seemed to disappear and reappear at will.

Jesus specifically told His disciples He was not a ghost and ate some fish to prove it (Luke 24:36-43). One time, the resurrected Jesus cooked breakfast on the beach (John 21) and on another occasion, He invited Thomas to touch the wounds in His hands and side (John 20:27). The resurrected body of Jesus was undeniably physical and yet had supernatural qualities that we would usually associate with a spirit. Could this wonderful blend of spiritual and physical be how it was for the first man and woman?

Of one life

Adam and Eve are called man and wife and are 'one flesh' or of 'one kind' or 'life' (Genesis 2:24). This is why in traditional Hebrew culture, the behaviour of the wife is reckoned the behaviour of the husband and vice versa, because they are considered to be one person (for example see Genesis 18 when Sarah laughs and Abraham is held to account). Eve is taken from Adam's side and mankind, in the first human being, is separated into male and female.

> " *We are invited to do the same and find our wholeness or completeness in God* "

In this sense, Eve is not created (she was already 'in' Adam) but both male and female are made when Adam is separated. It would be just as true to say that when God created the gender of 'female' woman when Eve was taken from Adam's side, God also made the gender 'male' of man. Her spirit is the same spirit God breathed into them before they were separated.

This is a spiritual mystery as well as a physical one and articulated wonderfully in the marriage covenant between a man and a woman. In Eden they were physically naked and yet clothed in spiritual harmony with each other together with God's Spirit. Who knows what wonders the first people knew and experienced in this heavenly unity?

Wholeness and The Sabbath

This original state of wholeness (relational harmony between mankind and God) is a spiritual/physical reality. The English word 'wholeness' is seldom used in our Bible translations, but we often see the word 'holy' which is rooted in the concept of 'wholeness'. When we look at the etymology or origins of the word 'holy' we find that it developed from an Anglo Saxon word 'hālig' meaning, 'uninjured, sound, healthy, entire, complete'. When we say 'hello' to one another it comes from the original word 'hale' which means wholeness or health.

So, when we greet one another like this we are basically saying 'I bless you with good health'. Often the emphasis of the word 'holy' revolves around concepts of 'divine', 'separate', and 'untouchable'. However, it also contains meanings of 'completeness' or 'wholeness'. I am not suggesting that this changes the definition of holiness, but that it adds another wonderful dimension to it. One of the reasons God is holy (Leviticus 11:44) is because He is perfectly whole or complete.

The first thing God declares holy in His entire creation is neither an object, an animal or a person, but a time:

"Thus the heavens and the earth were completed in all their vast array. By the seventh day God had finished the work he had been doing; so on the seventh day he rested from all his work. Then God blessed the seventh day and made it holy,

because on it he rested from all the work of creating that he had done." Genesis 2:2-3

There are some powerful truths in this Scripture. The first is that God considers holiness a blessing. The second is that although creation was 'completed' and God had seen that it was very good (Genesis 1:31), it was not fully holy (or we might say, 'whole') until He rested and it rested in Him. Therefore, one powerful meaning of Sabbath is that we are invited to do the same and receive our wholeness or completeness in God.

The power of selective vision

When Aliss and I were engaged to be married in 1988, I was amazed at how many TV programmes and magazines suddenly appeared on the subject of weddings. Everywhere I looked I saw books and programmes on weddings. Where had they all come from? I was sure they hadn't been there before.

Of course, the truth was, they had always been there and what had really changed was me. Because we were planning to get married, everything about weddings suddenly became important to me, and so that's what I saw. This phenomenon is called 'selective vision' and it means that I will primarily see, or select, things that are important to me and become 'blind' to the things that are not. The magazines and TV programmes on weddings disappeared after we were married, but recently as our daughter began planning her wedding, they all reappeared again!

When 'the eye' is mentioned in Scripture it often means much more than the physical organ we call an eye. The eye can also be a metaphor for our understanding, or the way we perceive; it's 'the window of the soul' if you like (Psalm 119:18, Proverbs 3:21, Matthew 5:8). This is why Jesus says in Matthew 6:22-23 that if your eyes are good then your whole body will be filled with light. It's not just *what* we see but the *way* we see which profoundly affects us.

How we see or perceive the world around us affects our most fundamental beliefs, including who we think God is (or if He exists at all), who we think we are, and therefore ultimately, how we live our lives. Jesus was saying that a good perception can bring us spiritual enlightenment that fills us with the life-giving revelation of God's truth. On the other hand, a bad perception can bring us a distorted view of the world, the kind of deception that breeds corruption, hatred and fear. How we see is determined by what we value in our hearts.

Pleasing to the eye

When the devil tempted Eve, he suggested to her that she should distrust God. We have already seen that the first manifestation of that temptation was the thought that the fruit of the tree of the knowledge of good and evil was 'good for food'. The second was to think that the fruit looked 'pleasing to the eye'.

> " *How we see is determined by what we value in our hearts* "

Now to be clear, 'good for food' was not a problem in itself and neither was enjoying the colours and shapes of all the other fruits of the garden. Genesis 2 tells us that God had filled the garden with an abundance of trees that were 'pleasing to the eye'. We are also reminded that the wonderful diversity of nature: the colours, sights and sounds of creation, are something to be enjoyed and celebrated because they testify to the glory of God (Psalms 104).

No, the real threat here was that mankind was entertaining the thought or temptation that *something God had prohibited* was 'pleasing to the eye' or 'desirable'. The temptation was distorting Eve's perception, and when perception becomes distorted by a mistrust of God's goodness it's called a deception. In his epistle, John calls this deception 'the lust of the eyes' because it gives birth to destructive desires.

It will make me more desirable

Look what was happening here: the object of perception (the fruit of the tree of the knowledge of good and evil) was being imbued with desirability in the 'eye' of the beholder. This desire came from a deception in the heart that imagined that the possession of the object would fulfil a need, and that need was to be more desirable. It's much like an expensive piece of diamond jewellery that may captivate me - I desire to possess it so that it will make me more captivating. I imagine that the beauty I see in the object will, if I possess it, increase my beauty.

This is tragic because once Adam and Eve had entertained the idea that they needed something additional to be more desirable to God, then they entertained the notion that God's perfect love for them could be increased. In turn, this convinced them that they *needed something they lacked* in order to be more desirable. This sin made them less valued than they truly were, or incomplete (we might say un-whole or unholy) in their own eyes.

Think of possessions you've craved in the past. Sometimes objects become 'needful things' don't they? I can think back to times when a comic book, or a music album or even a piece of clothing became a 'must have at any cost' item to me. On one level we know we're being obsessive or irrational but, like the character of Gollum in the Lord of the Rings story, desirable things so quickly become 'my precious'. We believe in some way that they're meeting a need in us and making us complete. However, more often than not, they are actually sucking the life out of us and our true identity is being lost in the object. We become pale shadows of who we really are.

It's an idolising worship that makes us exalt an object of desire in our own eyes and allows it to eclipse the place of God in our lives. Only in worshipping our creator God above all else do we become fulfilled in our need for love because only in Him are we fully accepted and loved.

The diagram below recaps the causal link between the temptations in the Garden of Eden and the curses subsequently released in the areas of provision and wholeness:

Temptation at the fall:	Sin committed when temptation acted upon:	Curse released by the sin:
Good for food	Doubt in God's provision for me	Famine (a lack of provision)
Pleasing to the eye	Doubt in God's love of me	Disease (a lack of wholeness)

Chapter Seven:
The Curse of Disease

"Which of you fathers, if your son asks for a fish, will give him a snake instead?" Luke 11:11

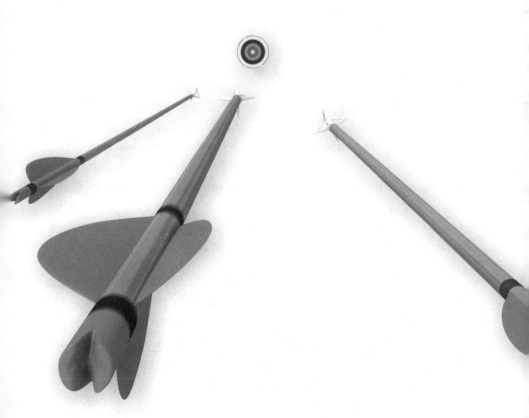

We have established from the Biblical narrative that when God created the first people, He created them perfectly whole and perfectly loved. There was no sickness. Often, I think we give sickness far too much credit and significance. We give it a grand sounding Latin name and speak of it with fear and reverence. But sickness or disease is simply a lack of wholeness. When we say, "I've got a cold" or "I've got a broken bone", what we essentially mean is that "I have lost my health" or "I have lost my wholeness".

When a broken bone gets healed the brokenness doesn't go anywhere, it simply ceases to exist. Even in the case of cancer, the tumour cannot live without the body. Many sicknesses are simply parasitic bacteria or viral parasites that expire without a host. Just as darkness is an absence of light, sickness is an absence of health. This is an important paradigm when we are ministering to the sick because we are not commanded to 'pray for the sickness' but to 'heal (or make whole) the sick' (Matthew 10:8). Yes, we may tell the sickness or brokenness to go but what use is that unless we tell the body or the tissue to be healthy.

A friend of mine called Sergio once prayed for a work colleague in his van during their lunch break. His colleague's ankle had metal pins holding the damaged bones together and it caused him a lot of pain. So, my friend stepped out in faith and commanded the metal pins to go. His colleague watched in horror as his ankle began to assume a strange and unnatural angle. He cried out, "What have you done to my ankle?!" Realising what was happening my friend answered, "Oh, I'm sorry… Bones reconstruct in Jesus name!"

He had removed the problem without providing the solution. Happily, not only was the ankle restored, but his colleague also received salvation (or we might say healing of the soul), praise God! So, we command the body to be whole or the tissue in the bone to be made new in Jesus' name. That's what it means to 'heal the sick'; we are ministers of wholeness.

Needful things

When Eve began to believe in her heart that the fruit of the tree of knowledge was 'pleasing to the eye' it became to her a needful thing. She believed it would somehow make her more desirable if it were possessed. As we have seen, this was a vain imagining because the first people simply could not be more desired and accepted by God. The immediate consequence of this deception is poignantly demonstrated by the first impact of sin upon them:

"Then the eyes of both of them were opened, and they realized they were naked; so they sewed fig leaves together and made coverings for themselves." Genesis 3:7

Through this act of mistrust in God's love, mankind stepped out of their God-given 'crown of glory and honour' (Psalm 8:5) and became 'self-centred' instead of 'God-centred'. Though the text, 'their eyes were opened' implies that their perception was increased, their reality had become carnal or physical and their spiritual perception, or their ability to perceive God rightly was greatly diminished.

The battle of the sexes

Not only did Adam and Eve abandon their wholeness in God through their unbelief in His perfect love but also their unity with each other. This is dramatically demonstrated by possibly the first marital row in history when Adam says of his wife, 'She made me do it!' He was evidently now thinking about 'me' instead of 'us'. The beautiful harmony that existed between the husband and wife was replaced by the curse over Eve: **'your desire shall be for your husband but he will rule over you...'** (Genesis 3:12).

Once again, this is not a random punishment dealt out by a whimsical God, but rather the manifest result of the sin relating to the temptation 'pleasing to the eye' which damages the whole sphere of human desire. Not only is their unity with God broken but also their unity with each other. What was once whole and united became broken and out of balance.

The fruit of union under the curse

The breaking of unity between the man and the woman manifests in pain. Just as the curse of lack manifested primarily with the man, the curse of pain and disunity manifests primarily in the woman. It's significant that the first mention of pain in the Scriptures is in the curse God spoke over Eve when He said, "**I will make your pains in childbearing very severe; with painful labour you will give birth to children.**" (Genesis 3:16). And so, despite the joy of childbirth, this miraculous event is a great time of crisis for both mother and child.

Statistics show that during the 19th century in England, about 5% of women are reckoned to have died in childbirth (*Journal of the Royal Society of Medicine*). That's one in twenty pregnant women regardless of how healthy they were; a mortality rate often remedied today by Caesarian section. Why is a natural process like childbirth such a crisis of life for both the mother and the baby? Why do so many women suffer from the pain of the menstrual cycle each month? Why this particular curse?

Genesis gives us the answer. It is because mankind rejected God's love and acceptance that they experienced separation and disunity. Because the desire between men and women became broken, the fruit of that desire, namely the birthing of children, manifested in pain. Also, we cannot ignore here that the significance of the sign of covenant (a promise of fruitfulness and blessing) between God and Israel was to be male circumcision, the seat of a man's sexual desire (an outward sign fulfilled by circumcision of the heart, the seat of the soul's desire, in the new covenant).

It's evident that we're not simply talking about the experience of women here, but how the whole of creation became subject to the cycle of life and death. Mankind's rejection of God was so cataclysmic that it bound nature into a fallen state of brokenness, subject to pain and decay until it would be set free and return to wholeness.

> " *Just as darkness is an absence of light, sickness is an absence of health* "

"For the creation was subjected to frustration, not by its own choice, but by the will of the one who subjected it, in hope that the creation itself will be liberated from its bondage to decay and brought into the freedom and glory of the children of God." Romans 8:20-21

Sexual desire

"And God blessed them. And God said to them, 'Be fruitful and multiply and fill the earth...'" Genesis 1:28

Though God ordained and blessed the reproduction of mankind before The Fall, we can say with some confidence that after The Fall the nature of sex and sexuality became profoundly altered. Just as other desires became primarily about physical satisfaction, rather than spiritual fulfilment, so sexual appetite became about gratifying selfish need.

Sex (the need for it and the promise of it) is a major power in our world today and always has been. Just as money encapsulates physical provision, the whole realm of sexuality in our world encapsulates our need to desire and be desired. Prostitution is hailed as one of the oldest professions in the world but since the 'sexual revolution' of the twentieth century the global sex industry has flourished. Rather than being the deeply spiritual and life sustaining part of marriage it was supposed to be, sex has become devalued, recreational and self-satisfying.

Fuelled by the ubiquitous use of the internet, society has witnessed a veritable explosion of global 'sexploitations': sex trafficking, prostitution, pornography, child abuse and cyber-sex which are all symptoms of this curse. Sexual deviance is commonplace and even celebrated in our western cultures, but the Bible teaches that sexuality is only truly redeemed into wholeness (holiness) when a husband and wife are united in spiritual as well as physical unity (Ephesians 5:31-32).

The gift of life

God's response to Adam and Eve's newfound physical awareness and shame is profoundly merciful. In Genesis 3 we witness the first sacrifice of an animal to 'cover' the nakedness of Adam and Eve:

"The Lord God made garments of skin for Adam and his wife and clothed them." Genesis 3:26

In this first act of propitiation, God took the life of an animal to provide a remedy for man's new state of exposure and vulnerability. This wasn't merely a physical provision to cover and help protect the physical body, but also a spiritual one, because it involved the taking of life and the shedding of blood. Throughout Scripture, physical blood is symbolic of life:

"For the life of a creature is in the blood, and I have given it to you to make atonement for yourselves on the altar; it is the blood that makes atonement for one's life." Leviticus 17:11

Though God had said that Adam and Eve would surely die if they ate from the tree of the knowledge of good and evil, it was an animal that first tasted death at God's hand. Before God sacrificed the animal, one of Adam and Eve's first responses to their new sense of carnality had been to sew fig leaves together and try to cover their nakedness. This use of vegetable life to attempt to compensate for a lack of righteousness, symbolises both legalism and licence.

On the one hand, the fact that they laboured with a 'needle and thread' to achieve this covering is an act of manmade (rather than God-ordained) religion; trying to appear right with God by one's own efforts. On the other hand, the use of vegetable life for escapism into drug and alcohol abuse has long been a way of relieving the pain that only reconciliation with God can remedy. Our pharmaceutical industries do much to relieve the suffering in our world through the amazing work of doctors and nurses, but even they would admit that they can't make people whole. Ultimately only God can do this work.

God rejects Cain's offering

This principal of propitiation is again reinforced in Genesis chapter 4 where we read how God was pleased with Abel's offering of a lamb but rejected Cain's offering of vegetables. Unity could only be restored through life blood. It may seem unfair and arbitrary to us that God rejected Cain's offering. The Bible is not explicit regarding the reason for Cain's wrong doing, but in the light of this truth about atonement, we can begin to understand why. Cain was the man who thought he deserved God's favour for all his hard 'works' in the garden and Abel re-enacted the God ordained principle of sacrificial grace.

Not only had Abel re-enacted the life blood propitiation established by God himself in Genesis 3:26 but he had also prophesied the atoning sacrifice of the Messiah. This act was so significant that Jesus himself called Abel the first prophet, pointing out that he had died for his obedience (Luke 11:50-51). God had already demonstrated to this first family that a return to wholeness in relationship with Him could only be reconciled through life blood. Even then, the covering blood of an animal would only be a temporary covering and one that would have to be repeated. Only when the Christ came, the Lamb of God who takes away the sin of the world, would mankind be restored to wholeness forever (Hebrews 9:13-14).

The curse of disease

We come across many Christians who have persuaded themselves that sickness is somehow a blessing. As far as I can see, this is usually achieved by combining a need to justify 'why I am not getting healed' with some strange theological acrobatics. However, the Scriptures clearly and emphatically designate sickness as a curse, and health as a blessing. Of course, God can use sickness for good ends but that doesn't make the sickness itself good, it only makes God good. It may seem obvious, but perhaps some of us need to start believing this scriptural truth: 'Health is good and sickness is bad'.

The very definition of sickness or disease is a lack of wholeness. In Deuteronomy 28: 21-61, there is a long list of curses such as plagues, fever, inflammation, boils, tumors and the like. It is evident that God does not consider sickness to be a blessing, but rather a curse. Sickness is essentially the absence of health and wholeness. Mankind suffered the loss of health and wholeness when we suffered the loss of our right relationship with God. It's out of this that all other forms of sickness and pain manifest for humanity and the whole world.

The place the sickness stopped

The life of King David is well known for many reasons, and most of them are good and honourable. However, he also made two major mistakes during his reign: the first cost him the life of his son and the second, the lives of 70,000 Israelites. His first and most notorious failing was committing adultery with the wife of Uriah the Hittite, a beauty called Bathsheba. He took her to his bed and, unable to persuade Uriah to sleep with her (to help cover his tracks), David had him murdered at the front lines. King David's second major error of judgement was that he took a census.

It may sound puzzling that a King should be considered sinful for taking a census of his own fighting men, but David should have known better. After all, David himself had written:

Psalm 33:16 "No king is saved by the size of his army; no warrior escapes by his great strength."

It was the sin of pride in human strength that he succumbed to and it brought shame on the whole nation. In 1 Chronicles 21 the prophet Gad told David:

"These are the choices the Lord has given you. You may choose three years of famine, three months of destruction by the sword of your enemies, or three days of severe plague as the angel of the Lord brings devastation throughout the land of Israel." 1 Chronicles 21:11-12

The three punishments offered to King David constituted the three seminal curses unleashed at The Fall: famine, war and sickness. David was deeply distressed at this terrible choice, but it was one which he had to make. Submitting to the punishment, he chose three days of plague, reasoning that he would rather fall into the hands of God than of men.

The Lord God sent the Angel of Death and a horrific plague crept across the nation. It was an angel the Lord had sent before, during the Israelite captivity in Egypt. But at that time, the Israelites had been protected by the blood of the Passover lamb. Now it was as if the Lord had lifted His covering protection from the people and thousands succumbed to the disease. Finally, just as the angel was preparing to devastate Jerusalem, the Lord could bear it no longer and cried **"Stop! That is enough!"** and the angel relented:

"David looked up and saw the angel of the Lord standing between heaven and earth with his sword drawn, reaching out over Jerusalem." 1 Chronicles 21:16

The place the angel had stopped in Jerusalem was a threshing floor belonging to a local farmer named Araunah. The prophet Gad instructed David to build an altar of thanksgiving there, and so the King offered to buy the land. At this, Araunah fell down and exclaimed that he would willingly give it to his sovereign, including the bulls, the wood and the wheat for the sacrifice. But David insisted that he would not offer the Lord that which had cost him nothing, so he bought the threshing floor with gold. David made the thanksgiving sacrifices to the Lord upon the new altar and they were burnt up by fire from heaven:

"Then the Lord spoke to the angel, who put the sword back into its sheath." 1 Chronicles 21:27

The threshing floor of Araunah is a highly significant place because not only was it the location where the plague stopped but it also became the site where David's son King Solomon built the Temple:

"Then Solomon began to build the temple of the LORD in Jerusalem on Mount Moriah, where the LORD had appeared to his father David. It was on the threshing floor of Araunah the Jebusite, the place provided by David." 2 Chronicles 3:1

The Temple in Jerusalem was founded on 'the place the sickness stopped'. It was a place of mercy and healing and wholeness. When Jesus was tempted by the devil for the second time, it was no accident that this was the very place His adversary chose for the battle.

Temptation at the fall:	Sin committed:	Curse released:	Blessing to Israel:
Pleasing to the eye	Doubt in God's love of me	Disease and pain	The temple is 'the place the sickness stopped'

Chapter Eight:
The Blessing of Wholeness

"May God himself, the God who makes everything
holy and whole, make you holy and whole,
put you together - spirit, soul, and body."
1 Thessalonians 5:23-24 MSG

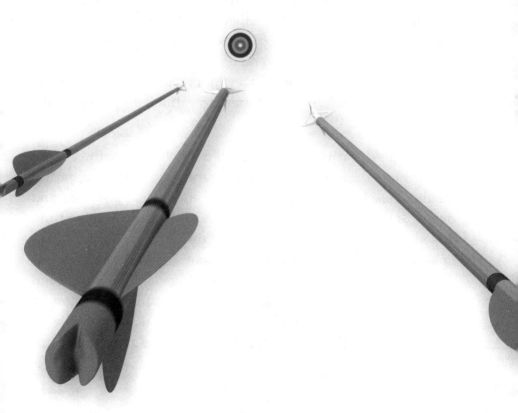

Dirctly before Jesus went into the wilderness He had been baptised by John and received both the anointing of the Holy Spirit and the blessing of His Heavenly Father:

"the Holy Spirit descended on him in bodily form like a dove. And a voice came from heaven: 'You are my Son, whom I love; with you I am well pleased.'" Luke 3:22

This statement, **"You are my Son, whom I love; with you I am well pleased"** was part of a rite of passage for a Jewish boy who came of age and was ready to help in his father's business. The father would take the young man to the market square and would announce to the other traders and the public that this was his son in whom he placed every confidence. In effect, he was saying to the community, 'From now on, when you do business with my son, then you do business with me.' It was an incredibly important affirmation of the father's trust and love for his child. For those who heard God's public declaration at the baptism of Jesus there would have been no doubt as to its meaning. This is not unlike God's affirmation over Adam and Eve when He saw that creation **"was very good and He validated it completely"** (Genesis 1:31 AMP).

Desiring approval is deeply etched into human nature. Every child wants the approval of their parents, students the approval of their teacher, employees of their employer, husbands and wives of their spouses. We want to know that we are valued and loved. Psychologists maintain that this is essential for us to mature and grow into the fullness of knowing who we are[1]. In our lives, there are countless voices clamouring to fulfil this need and give us their approval. However, as we all know, human approval is often flawed and unreliable, and it's only God who can fully meet this need. At His baptism, Jesus received this

---

1. Developmental psychologists in studies such as 'We are by nature Social Beings' William Glasser, 'We become ourselves through others' Lev Vygotsky, 'Early Emotional bonds are an integral part of human nature' John Bowlby

approval from His Heavenly Father and it became the foundation of who He was and all that He did.

The second temptation:
The arena of love and acceptance

The devil does a curious thing in his next temptation of Jesus:

"Then the devil took him to the holy city and had him stand on the highest point of the temple." Matthew 4:5

We may wonder what Jesus was doing allowing the devil to take Him anywhere. However, we must remember that it was the Holy Spirit who had led Jesus into the wilderness for a time of testing and God was allowing the devil to tempt Him. The devil had demonstrated supernatural power and transported Jesus bodily from the wilderness to the top of the Temple in Jerusalem.

> " *At His baptism Jesus received this approval from His Heavenly Father and it became the foundation of who He was and all that He did* "

To Israel, the Temple Mount was one of the holiest places in the world. Many scholars believe that the 'pinnacle of the Temple' may have been a building which overlooked the precipice of the valley below making a frightening 450-foot drop (the equivalent of a 45-story building). We can say with some certainty that Jesus was transported bodily here because of the temptation which followed:

'"If you are the Son of God," he said, "throw yourself down. For it is written:

'He will command his angels concerning you, and they will

lift you up in their hands, so that you will not strike your foot against a stone.'"' Matthew 4:6

It is true to say that strictly speaking, the temptations of Jesus did not all take place in the wilderness. The temptation of provision took place in the wilderness, but then the temptation to doubt His Father's love for him took place on the Temple in Jerusalem, the epicentre of religious power. In the previous temptation, Jesus had successfully overcome the devil by quoting Scripture at Him. And now, just like a professional fighter, the devil adjusted his strategy to adapt to the fighting style of his adversary. In a stroke of combative genius, the devil began to quote Scripture too.

Psalm 91: 'Heavenly medicine'

The devil made a falsehood when he tempted Eve to eat the forbidden fruit by mixing truth with lies, and he used the same tactic here by quoting Scripture in a crafty way. It's obvious that 'knowing Scripture' doesn't make us any closer to God if our hearts are against Him.. We must also know the one of whom the Scriptures testify (John 5:39). The devil's quote of '**He will command his angels concerning you...**' comes from Psalm 91 which speaks of God's protective anointing for those who live in His presence. In its entirety, Psalm 91 is one of the most wonderfully comforting Psalms, particularly for those who are suffering from sickness or the threat of disease. Verses 3 and 4 of this Psalm declare:

"Surely he will save you from the fowler's snare and from the deadly pestilence. He will cover you with his feathers, and under his wings you will find refuge."

Charles Spurgeon said this of Psalm 91: 'In the whole collection there is not a more cheering Psalm, its tone is elevated and sustained throughout, faith is at its best, and speaks nobly. A

German physician was wont to speak of it as the best preservative in times of cholera, and in truth, it is a heavenly medicine against plague and pest.'[2]

It seems from his choice of Scripture, the devil was fully aware that this battle was being fought out in the arena of health and wholeness. He had already succeeded in tempting Eve to question the extent of God's love for her and that had resulted in the curse of pain and disunity being released. Now he attempts to lead Jesus into the same sin by the same temptation of questioning His Heavenly Father's love for Him.

Does your Father really love you?

Again, Jesus refused to be drawn in and simply settled the issue by quoting another command from the Scriptures:

"Jesus answered him, 'It is also written: 'Do not put the Lord your God to the test.'" Matthew 4:7

If Jesus had continued to quote from this passage in Deuteronomy He would also have added: '**...as you did at Massah,**' (Deuteronomy 6:16) directly associating His testing in the wilderness with that of the Israelites. The Scripture refers to a time when God's people were suffering from thirst so badly, they were about to stone Moses to death (Exodus 17:4). The place name Massah means 'testing' or 'temptation' and the people were so wretched they began to say: **"Is the Lord among us or not?"** (Exodus 17:7).

The devil was effectively saying to Jesus, 'Is the Lord with you or not? If you are the Son of God why don't you prove it...? If you do something to hurt or endanger yourself then your Father will surely come and save you, won't He? This will both prove His love and your divinity.' He was tempting Jesus to employ the tactic of a petulant child who throws a tantrum to gain his

2. The Treasury of David by Charles H Spurgeon © public domain

parent's attention. Such a child might throw himself down to manipulate the parent's expressions of love and care.

Both the devil and Jesus knew they were standing in a place of judgement and execution for religious heretics. It was a brutal custom for those deemed blasphemers to be hurled from this temple roof top. If Jesus were to be supernaturally rescued from His fall in front of the Temple, then His divine credentials would be established forever. The religious community would surely receive Him as their promised Messiah.

This was the type of sign the Jewish religious leaders often asked Jesus to perform throughout His ministry (John 6:30, Matthew 12:38). However, Jesus would not be drawn; His position was fixed, He did not need to test His Father. He would simply accept and believe by faith that His Father was with Him and loved Him fully. Jesus knew He was wholly accepted and did not need to act out of insecurity to receive this love and affirmation.

Jesus would have known the message of Psalm 91 well; it is only by trusting in God's faithfulness that we find true refuge and protection. I wonder if the devil was aware that the portion of the Psalm he quoted ends with this promise:

"You will tread on the lion and the cobra; you will trample the great lion and the serpent." Psalm 91:13

And so, Jesus found Himself back in the wilderness having passed the second test.

Temptation at the fall:	Sin committed:	Curse released:	Jesus' temptation in the wilderness:
Good for food	Doubt in God's provision for me	Famine (a lack of provision)	Turn these stones into bread
Pleasing to the eye	Doubt in God's love of me	Disease (a lack of health)	Throw yourself from the temple top

Chapter Nine:
Living from Sonship

"I will not leave you as orphans; I will come to you."
John 14:18

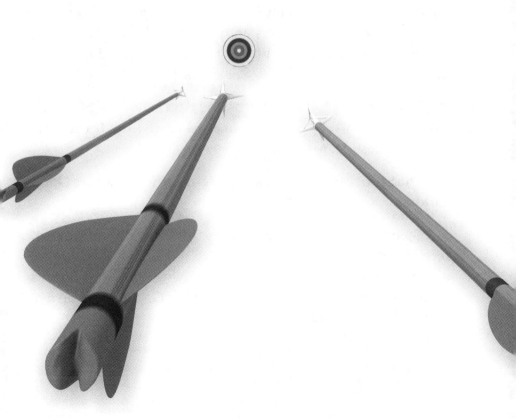

Our deep seated need to be loved and accepted can manifest in all kinds of destructive-compulsive behaviours. These can cause us to manipulate the affections of others through aggressive or passive coercion, often without us even realising it, and in extreme cases these relationships can even become abusive. For many, the need to be affirmed can also lead to activities that are superficially good but are driven by the same need. For example, compensating for low self-esteem by over-working, obsessive serving, or even, dare I say it, 'doing ministry'.

Not only do we need the Word of God in our lives but we also need the presence and power of the Holy Spirit. In the first chapter of Colossians, Paul prays for the believers that God would fill them with **"the knowledge of his will through all the wisdom and understanding that the Spirit gives"** (Colossians 1:9). Immersing ourselves in Scripture is only beneficial if we have the Holy Spirit to give us the spiritual understanding we need to apply it. Then, we are promised that we will bear fruit in every good work and grow in the knowledge of God (Colossians 1:10-11).

The Holy Spirit is the person of God who makes adoption into God's family not only possible, but also known to us, because He constantly testifies to that reality:

"The Spirit himself testifies with our spirit that we are God's children." Romans 8:16

When we live out of insecurity it's because we are not receiving that testimony of sonship[1]; we are behaving as if we are orphans. It's only by constantly receiving the Holy Spirit's affirmation that we are loved and belong to God that we can live from a place of security.

---

1. The term sonship here is meant figuratively and applies to both male and female genders (just as men are included in the collective term 'Bride of Christ').

The new wine of the Spirit

The Scripture: **"Do not get drunk on wine, which leads to debauchery. Instead, be filled with the Spirit,"** (Ephesians 5:18) highlights an antithesis between drunkenness and being filled with the Spirit - a similarity that caused the error made by onlookers when the Spirit was first poured out (Acts 2:15). This is because being filled with the Spirit is a kind of divine intoxication that is wonderfully liberating, joyous and empowering.

If we desire to know how to be filled with the Spirit and experience this heavenly joy then we need look no further than the next verse: **"...speaking to one another with psalms, hymns, and songs from the Spirit. Sing and make music from your heart to the Lord, always giving thanks to God the Father for everything, in the name of our Lord Jesus Christ."** (Ephesians 5:19-20). The key to being continually filled with the Spirit is to have a lifestyle of worship. This is more than simply singing Christian songs, it's **'always giving thanks to God the Father for everything'**, or having a heart constantly turned towards God.

My wife Aliss has one of the most powerful healing ministries I know of, but it doesn't happen in a vacuum because Aliss also has one of the closest relationships with the Holy Spirit I know of too. After hearing her speak of that relationship, many are so impacted by it that they ask her, "How can I have a relationship with the Holy Spirit like you do?" And she will tell them that it's really no secret. She invests time in that relationship. She speaks with the Holy Spirit and listens to Him as well. And most importantly she is sensitive to His direction, always trying to hear His voice and obey Him quickly. It's a lifestyle of worship, of a heart turned towards God. That's it really – simple.

An attitude of worship and thankfulness makes us attentive to the direction of the Holy Spirit. It's a lifestyle that makes us alive to the miraculous possibilities of God in every moment. Just talk to God right now and thank him for His presence with you and see what happens. It's as if you just 'came back into the room' or 'entered into the present'. It's one of the unquestioning child-like qualities that Jesus said was essential for entering the Kingdom of God (see Matthew 18:2-4).

Remember, it's through the testimony of the Holy Spirit that we receive our Father God's affirmation that we are beloved children. And it's from this deep-seated identity that we can experience **'the peace of God that transcends all understanding'** (Philippians 4:7).

Healing in the blood

An important part of worship is the observation of The Lord's Supper or Communion. As we pass the one cup, the wine we share is a powerful symbol of the Lord's blood poured out for us. It's through the cross that we are set free from the curse of sickness and death and brought into the freedom and blessing of wholeness. The wine is particularly symbolic of this aspect of the threefold blessing because it represents both the bitterness of sin and the joy of life. When you drink the cup with others, thank the Lord for the blessing of healing and wholeness that flows from the cross.

I began by saying how our need for affirmation can drive us into a performance orientated life. True worship is the remedy for that malady because it helps us to stop and be still, not just on the outside, but on the inside as well. Just as Jesus proved His obedience to the Holy Spirit and had no doubt in His Father's love and affirmation, so too must we. It's in the knowledge of sonship that we enter into the Sabbath rest of God. And I believe it's from this life-spring of wholeness that His supernatural healing power may flow through us to restore others.

Third Blessing:
Authority

Chapter Ten:
Subjected to Slavery

"Stand firm, then, and do not let yourselves
be burdened again by a yoke of slavery."
Galatians 5:1

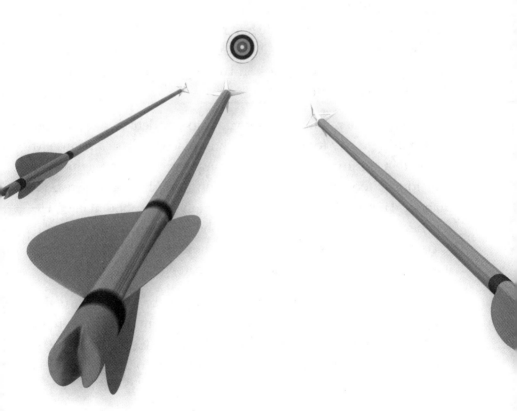

After the Lord had steered us through our financial crisis and we were on a more even keel, He then asked Aliss to give up her well-paid career and our dream home, and subsequently to set up an outreach programme in the nearby neighbourhood of Blacon. He gave her a deep compassion for this social housing community which had gained a notorious reputation for crime, drugs, poor health and unemployment. We couldn't even drive through it without her bursting into tears. It was a large housing estate on the route between our village and the city of Chester, so the tears came regularly.

I remember evenings when she would be so emotional and upset that I could hardly get any sense out of her. It was a heady mixture of excitement at what God was going to do, love for the people and, to my consternation, a conviction that I was going to be involved as well! (At the time, I led a home group for our local church, but had no aspiration to be a pastor or get involved in outreach). That last one made her giggle because I just shook my head in disbelief and said that it would never happen. I ended up phoning some trusted friends and saying, "Can we come over? I don't know what to do with her."

Sometime later, after we'd moved into our debt free home and were getting ready to plant a church in Blacon, Aliss came face to face with a spiritual principality that appeared on our neighbour's roof top. It took the form of a person and she could sense its diabolical nature. When she asked the Holy Spirit about it later, He told her it was, 'The Prince of Blacon'. She didn't sense any direction to confront it 'head on' but to simply ignore it. We knew the reason it was manifesting was because it felt threatened.

Our mandate was clear, we were to 'preach the good news of the Kingdom of God, heal the sick and cast out demons'. We were to worship Jesus in word and action and the Lord would take care of the evil principality. We were not to be distracted or intimidated.

I tell this story at the beginning of a chapter on authority because there is a strong connection in the Kingdom of God between compassion and authority. God will rarely give us true power and authority where there is not true love and compassion. The purpose of miracles in the new covenant is ultimately to manifest God's love and power to a people He desires to know Him; you can't have one without the other (see 1 Corinthians 14:1).

Good beginnings

"When God created mankind, he made them in the likeness of God. He created them male and female and blessed them. And he named them "Mankind" (or Adam) when they were created." Genesis 5:1-2

In this verse we read that when God created mankind, He made them in His *likeness*. This is the same language as is used in the term, 'according to their kinds', so that just as sheep beget lambs or little sheep, so God created 'little gods'; those who are of His image and nature (Psalm 82:6 and John 10:34).

There is no account of God breathing His life-giving breath into any other creature He made in the same way He did with mankind: **"Then the Lord God formed [that is, created the body of] man from the dust of the ground, and breathed into his nostrils the breath of life; and the man became a living being [an individual complete in body and spirit]." Genesis 2:7 AMP**

In Genesis 2 we see an intimate bond formed between God and mankind when Adam was brought to life out of a 'face to face' and 'breath to breath' exchange with his maker. There is a fundamental connection between this bond and our authority over the earth. In Genesis 1 verse 26 we read: **"Then God said, "Let us make mankind in our image, in our likeness, *so that they may rule over...*"** (Italics added). **"Let us make man in our image",** Why? **"So that they may rule over…"**

> **" God will rarely give us true power and authority where there is not true love and compassion "**

Our God-given mandate to 'rule over the earth' or 'take care of it rightly' is subject to our very nature of being godlike and made in His image. Many Christians shy away from such language because it seems prideful or presumptuous, but the message of the Bible is that Jesus came to restore this divine condition. In the fourth century, Athanasius of Alexandria summed up the principle like this:

'For he became human that we might become divine; he revealed himself in a body that we might understand the unseen Father; he endured men's insults that we might inherit immortality' (extract from 'On the Incarnation').

I have said you are gods

Colossians chapter 1 states that Jesus is the very image of the living God. He is the perfect representation of His nature in the form of a man. When threatened with execution for saying He was the Son of God, in His defence Jesus quoted **Psalm 82:6: " Is it not written in your Law, 'I have said you are 'gods'?" John 10:34**. He was reminding the people of who they were originally created to be and how far they had fallen from the divine state. He was telling them that He was the gateway back to this eternal life.

Perhaps for many who accept the mystery of the incarnation, that Jesus was and is fully God as well as fully man, a greater challenge is to truly believe in our own participation in the divine nature. However, this was always the goal of the incarnation; that Jesus would be the *first born* of many:

"For those God foreknew he also predestined to be conformed to the image of his Son, that he might be the *firstborn* among many brothers and sisters." Romans 8:29 (Italics added).

This divine life is made possible by adoption into God's family through faith in Jesus:

"Through these he has given us his very great and precious promises, so that through them you may participate in the divine nature." 2 Peter 1:4

The Scriptures begin with the inauguration of mankind's godly authority but they also end with it. Revelation speaks of those who pay the ultimate price for their faith in Jesus being given, not only eternal life, but also the authority to rule over the earth in the Millennium (Revelation 20:4). We were created for the rewarding and purposeful work of ruling and reigning in godliness.

The temptation of the pride of carnal life

"When the woman saw that the fruit of the tree was good for food and pleasing to the eye, *and also desirable for gaining knowledge*, she took some and ate it." Genesis 3:6 (Italics added).

The third manifestation of the original temptation was the idea that the fruit of the tree of the knowledge of good and evil was desirable for gaining knowledge; in other words, 'if I eat this fruit it will make me *more powerful*'. This was surely the rebellion of the devil when he presumed to raise himself up in pride to be like God (Isaiah 14:14). The devil knew that he was doomed to the fires of hell for such a treasonable act and so he had, in his dreadful bitterness, determined to take these 'little-god creatures' down with him.

Though we are created to be god-like we are not created to *be* God or take His place. Though God is benevolent in so many wonderful ways there are aspects to His nature that we were never created to experience. One of these unique attributes is possessing 'the knowledge of good and evil'. On the face of it this may seem like good knowledge to have. After all, if we know what is good and what is evil we can surely make better choices. But we can only come to that conclusion by seeing this knowledge from this side of the Fall. Before the Fall there was no weighing of right and wrong, or good and bad, there was only love, trust and unity.

Eating the fruit of 'the tree of the knowledge of good and evil' was partaking of an existence outside of, or separate from God. This is a knowledge which destroys us because it is analogous with experiencing an existence outside of life itself. It is then that our eyes fall upon ourselves in wonder, like the fabled Narcissus who fell in love with his own image. We become self-important, boastful and proud. But it's only when we live fully within the life of God, and eat only from 'the tree of life' (which represents Jesus), that we truly become like gods in the created order. The paradox is that when we do this we have no value or notion of our own divine nature because all we perceive and value is the Lord God Himself.

Delegated authority

'No man ruleth safely but that he is willingly ruled' (The Imitation of Christ – Thomas À Kempis).

Ultimately all power comes from God because He is the highest power and allows or withholds all power. It's important for us to understand the word 'delegated'. It means to entrust a task or responsibility to another person, typically one who is less senior than oneself. It also means to send or authorise (someone) to do something as a representative. So when **"God blessed them and said to them... 'Rule over the fish in the sea and the birds in the sky and over every living creature that moves on the ground,'"** (Genesis 1:28), He was delegating, entrusting and authorising us as His representatives with the responsibility of this work.

That's why it was Adam's task to name the animals and birds (see Genesis 2:20). Names are an extremely important part of our identity; that by which we are known and know others has a profound impact on our lives. I believe the naming of the animals and birds by Adam was a rite of passage for the God-given authority he received in Genesis 1:28. Adam's first sovereign act over the animals was bestowing the honour of titles over his subjects. It brought them into right and meaningful relationship with mankind and therefore with God.

True authority comes from above

The nature of true authority is that it comes from above (John 19:11). It's an altogether different state to have true authority than to simply have power. Power can be taken by violence and can force people who are weaker to do what it wants through fear and punishment. Conversely, true authority serves those it rules over. Self-appointed power is self-serving and self-seeking; it's the spirit behind all bullying and manipulation from the playground to the government.

Behind the serpent's apparent willingness to empower mankind was a subtle power play to take Adam's crown of authority for himself. In that single act of eating the forbidden fruit, Adam and Eve disobeyed God and submitted to the devil. In this act, they became subservient to the devil because they elevated his word above God's. In doing so, they effectively worshipped the devil and abdicated their earthly throne to him[1].

Because they fell to the temptation that the forbidden fruit would bring them more power and significance than God had already given them, they became disempowered and the servant of another master. Within this new world hierarchy, from a carnal perspective, power would now have to be gained by force and self-promotion. Some people may be born into privilege, but even then, that power would have to be maintained by political and military force. As one of Shakespeare's characters famously says, "Some are born great, some achieve greatness, and some have greatness thrust upon 'em"[2].

1. It's for this reason that the devil is often referred to by Jesus as 'the prince (or ruler) of this world' (John 12:31) and the Apostle Paul calls him 'the god of this world' (2 Corinthians 4:4).
2. Twelfth Night by William Shakespeare

Though a few found a better way through the desire to truly know God, most would remain subject to the pecking order of society. The very first story after the creation account is that of how Cain kills Abel as aggression and murder manifested between brothers. Tribe would war against tribe and nation against nation. The curse of war has blighted the history of mankind as one nation has risen through military might to become an Empire until it was inevitably torn down by another to take its place.

The battle of the ages

Many people suppose that the battle of the ages is between God and the devil, between the angelic hosts and the demonic hordes in an epic contest of good versus evil. But that is not where the primary war plays out. Far closer to the Biblical narrative is the battle between mankind and the devil; that is the real struggle of the ages. It was at the Fall that humankind was defeated and enslaved to the devil's despotism and we have struggled to break free from the yoke of sin and death ever since.

Jesus told us that the fires of hell were prepared, not primarily for mankind, but for the devil and his angels (Matthew 25:41). As in any earthly battle, the destiny of those belonging to each side is determined by the destiny of their commander in chief. If he falls, they all fall, and so it is in the spiritual (Matthew 13:38, 1 John 3:10). The Gospel tells us that the only remedy is to be yoked to the glorious destiny of our Lord Jesus Christ (Romans 8:17).

This subjection to our adversary is shown most powerfully by the curse spoken over the serpent which defines his relationship with humankind. God declared:

> **"And I will put enmity between you and the woman,**
> **and between your offspring and hers;**
> **he will crush your head, and you will strike his heel."**
> **Genesis 3:15**

The physical heel of a person is a symbol of their stability, thus striking the heel is a metaphor meaning to topple the whole person. Despite the best attempts of a man or woman to be strong in conflict, the poisonous strike of a snake to the heel will bring down the toughest hero. However, there is also blessing hidden in the curse over the serpent because the Scripture says that the offspring or seed of the woman will crush his head.

Many Bible scholars agree that even here, at the beginning of the human tragedy, we see a prophetic reference to the Messiah who would come in time to break the chains of the curse. Furthermore, one of the unique characteristics of death by crucifixion was that it bruised the victim's heal. Because humankind had abdicated their throne of authority, only the Son of Man could take it back. Even at the point of total loss and shame, God already had a plan of redemption for His beloved.

Israel and the blessing of true authority

The books of 1 and 2 Samuel tell the story of Israel's rise to power on the international stage through the lives and times of King Saul, King David and King Solomon. The story of Saul plays out like a Greek tragedy, when after good, humble beginnings and a heart to serve God, Saul fell foul of human insecurities. Initially Saul treated the boy David as one of his own sons; he invited him to live in the royal household and minister to the King with his harp and song. However, when David defeated the champion Goliath, the people began to sing David's praises:

> " *When those close to us receive promotion or adulation it often reveals what is in our hearts* "

"As they danced, they sang: 'Saul has slain his thousands, and David his tens of thousands.'" 1 Samuel 18:7

When those close to us receive promotion or adulation it often reveals what is in our hearts. For Saul, this was an opportunity, like a good father, to be proud of David and work with his adopted son to establish a great Kingdom. Instead, Saul exhibited deep paranoia and began to see David as a threat to his crown and dynasty. The rest of Saul's life is a moral tale on the futility of holding onto illegitimate power through fear and force. After many failed attempts to kill David, Saul finally ended up in a deep dark place; in the house of a witch. It is here that his imminent and untimely death was accurately foretold.

The worshipping king

By contrast, David took an entirely different approach to his call to power. Reading the Biblical narrative, humanly speaking, it's as if he seemed to sabotage every opportunity that presented itself to him to take power, even to the point of promoting his enemies. He held onto power so lightly that he was willing to walk away from it at any time. Even when his own son Absalom forced David to take up arms against him, in stark contrast to Saul, David ordered his men not to lay a hand on him. After the rebellion was put down David was so devastated his son had been slain in the battle that he refused to celebrate the victory. Consequently Joab, his own General, was compelled to rebuke David for making his army feel so ashamed (2 Samuel 19:1-8).

This is not to say that David was not a passionate and courageous fighter; on the contrary, he was a formidable warrior and surrounded by mighty men of great renown (1 Chronicles 11). But one of his core values was that God **"guides the humble in what is right and teaches them his way."** (Psalm 25:9). King David passionately believed that to have true authority was to submit to, or come under, the authority of God. As a consequence, the favour and power with which God anointed David didn't only affect his earthly life, but reached way beyond it into the eternal destiny of the world. Isaiah prophesied of the coming Messiah:

"For to us a child is born, to us a son is given, and the government will be on his shoulders. And he will be called Wonderful Counselor, Mighty God, Everlasting Father, Prince of Peace. Of the greatness of his government and peace there will be no end. He will reign on David's throne and over his kingdom, establishing and upholding it with justice and righteousness from that time on and forever. The zeal of the Lord Almighty will accomplish this." Isaiah 9:6-7

Temptation at the fall:	Sin committed:	Curse released:	Blessing to Israel:
Desirable for gaining knowledge	Doubt in God's authority over me (and my significance)	Slavery or subjugation to God's enemies	The reign of King David establishes an eternal throne

Chapter Eleven:
Supernatural Authority

"To the one who is victorious and does my will to the end, I will give authority over the nations."
Revelation 2:26

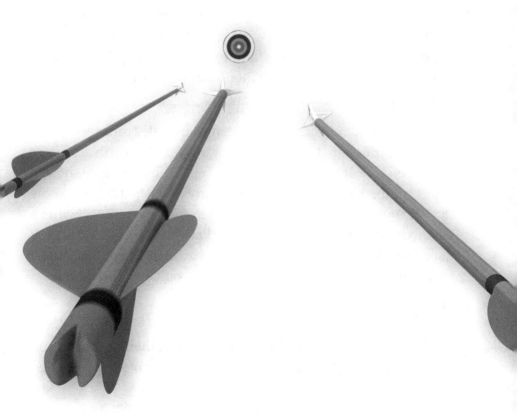

The third temptation: The arena of authority

The obedience of Jesus to His Heavenly Father was tested in the wilderness by a prince who had taken power by devious means. The devil's third temptation of Jesus is perhaps the most blatant attempt to exult himself. He showed Jesus the nations of the world:

"Again, the devil took him to a very high mountain and showed him all the kingdoms of the world and their splendor. 'All this I will give you,' he said, 'if you will bow down and worship me.'" Matthew 4:8-9

In spiritual and earthly matters 'high places' are often indicative of power and authority. Noah's Ark rested on Mount Ararat after the flood, Moses was given the Ten Commandments on Mount Sinai, Elijah heard the voice of God on Mount Horeb, and Mount Zion is where King David built Jerusalem. The wilderness had been the battleground for provision and the Temple in the Holy City for faith in His Heavenly Father's love. Finally, the setting of the high mountain was the battleground for authority over the nations of the world.

There is no doubt that this temptation appealed directly to Jesus' messianic mission to rule and reign over the earth as God's Anointed One. It is difficult for us to imagine how the devil showed Jesus 'all the kingdoms of the world' in one instant but we know that it must have been breathtaking in its scope. The devil is a shrewd and highly intelligent being (Ephesians 6:11), and as such he was almost certainly tempting Jesus to use this incredible power and authority for good, even though this would have been futile.

The devil's authority

The devil said to Jesus, **"I will give you all their authority and splendor; it has been given to me, and I can give it to anyone I want to." Luke 4:6**

Who gave this authority over the earth to the devil? The nations did not exist when Adam and Eve abdicated their right to rule and reign, but in that one act of idolatry they legally became the devil's subjects. The authority and splendour of the kingdoms of the world belong to the devil because they were all 'in' Adam when he bowed the knee.

It's significant that the devil was acknowledging that Jesus was not part of that transaction; his offer recognised that Jesus held a special place of authority outside of that subservience. That is why Jesus, and only Jesus, can 'rescue us from the dominion of darkness' (Colossians 1:13).

It's hard to believe the gall of the devil to come out with such a blatant offer as 'I'll trade worship for nations'. Perhaps he had exhausted the crafty approach and was now just cutting to the quick. He was effectively saying, 'OK Jesus, enough of the small talk, let's get down to some serious business; these nations of people are what it's all about.' This tells us that the devil values himself far more than he values the world. Perhaps he imagined that this act might save him from the fires of hell?

We don't know at this point whether the devil was aware of the road that lay ahead for Jesus, to the torture and execution at Golgotha. The devil evidently knew the Scriptures, and he knew that Jesus' destiny as the Messiah was to sit on David's throne forever. What the devil must have suspected was that he was offering Jesus a short cut to becoming King of Kings. However, Jesus knew better and was resolute:

"Jesus said to him, 'Away from me, Satan! For it is written: 'Worship the Lord your God, and serve him only.'" Matthew 4:10

A simple offer and a simple answer. The devil soon realised that where Adam and Eve had catastrophically failed, Jesus had gloriously succeeded. The battle was over. Jesus had proved himself a worthy champion. The narrative in Luke 4 says that when the devil had finished his tempting of Jesus, he left Him until an opportune time. We can't begin to conceive the desolation and rage the devil must have known at this ignominious defeat. His mind must have reeled with the anticipation of the damage Jesus was about to inflict on his dark kingdom. All his senses were now focussed upon this one man: He must be destroyed at all costs.

> "*Where Adam and Eve had catastrophically failed, Jesus had gloriously succeeded*"

Complete victory

Temptation at the fall:	Sin committed:	Curse released:	Jesus' temptation in the wilderness:
Good for food	Doubt in God's provision for me	Famine (a lack of provision)	Turn these stones into bread
Pleasing to the eye	Doubt in God's love of me	Disease (a lack of health)	Throw yourself from the temple top
Desirable for gaining knowledge	Doubt in God's authority over me	War (a lack of peace)	Worship the prince of this world

Jesus had maintained trust in His Heavenly Father and submitted to Him in all three arenas of provision, wholeness and authority. On all three counts, Jesus had stood firm and declared that, no matter what, He would trust in His Heavenly Father by faith and not by externals outside of God's provision, love and power. As in all other aspects of life, Jesus leads the way for us to follow.

"Then the devil left him, and angels came and attended him." Matthew 4:11

I've sometimes imagined this scene as golden haired angelic beings with wings and white cloaks lifting up the tired body of Jesus into a heavenly cloud, but on reflection I don't think it was that at all. After all, the angels (messengers) that appear in the Bible often appear as plain men (Hebrews 13:2). I believe it far more likely that the angels who attended to Jesus appeared as shepherds or nomads who gave Him shelter and food. I think that's a wonderful picture. A company of Arabic men leading camels bearing baggage and food gradually appear through the sun-baked haze. They make a camp and take Him in, providing Him with the food, love and honour that He always knew His Heavenly Father would supply.

Let's not be tempted to 'over-spiritualise' God's answers to our needs. Aliss and I can testify that during our times of hardship or trouble it has often been the kindness of family and friends bringing us meals, gift bags or even money, that has kept us going and got us through. These are often our attending angels or miracles. Sometimes God will send us answers in ways that we don't expect or recognise. They may not come as the epic, earth shattering displays of power that we might imagine, but with the wisdom of hindsight, perhaps they are.

Chapter Twelve:
Living in the Miraculous

"'If you can'?" said Jesus. "Everything is possible for one who believes." Mark 9:23

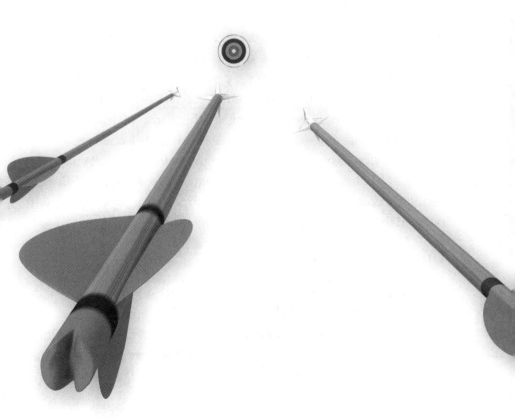

Somebody once said that if you only have the Bible without the power of the Holy Spirit then you dry up. On the other hand, if you have the Holy Spirit without the Bible then you blow up! But when we have the living Word of God and the Holy Spirit together then we grow up. It's the Word and the Spirit together that give us the maturity we need to move in true spiritual authority. The Word brings heaven to earth and the Holy Spirit connects earth with heaven. It's in this heaven and earth union that the supernatural manifests and we can begin to expect miracles.

I believe that the real need today in the lives of believers who desire to see God's manifest power is not primarily to have faith, but courage (because in truth, these two often partner together):

"Be on your guard; stand firm in the faith; be courageous; be strong." 1 Corinthians 16:13

It takes courage to ask a stranger who is sick or injured if you can pray for them. It takes courage to tell someone that their debilitating condition is simply a demon and they can be free of it. It takes courage to then cast it out, (even as others watch on) and minister forgiveness and healing in the name of Jesus. It takes courage to share a word of knowledge with a work colleague when you really don't know for sure if it's right. Faith is risky. 'What if I'm wrong? What if they reject me? What if I look foolish?' But no healing miracle, nor deliverance, nor supernatural provision will happen through us without faith and courage.

Unity in diversity

We all have the same Holy Spirit living in us, but God has made us all different. Aliss and I have very different personalities and we express the life of God in our own individual ways. I learned a long time ago that I can't be Aliss and I shouldn't try to be. God has made us all different for a reason and He delights in diversity.

You are unique, you are the best you there is, only you are alive at this time and in the place God has put you. We are all called to live out of the Spirit's supernatural love and power, but we do it in a way that flows through our own uniqueness. Look at how different Jesus' 12 disciples were, and yet they were all called to live lives overflowing with the miraculous:

> " _The Word brings heaven to earth and the Holy Spirit connects earth with heaven_ "

"Heal the sick, raise the dead, cleanse those who have leprosy, drive out demons. Freely you have received; freely give." Matthew 10:8

It strikes me that each of the disciples would have expressed that miraculous life in very different ways, but the power was all from the same Holy Spirit (1 Corinthians 12:11). Peter would act first and think later, Thomas would think first and act later, Simon the zealot was a political activist, Matthew an accountant, while the two Jesus called "sons of thunder" suggests they were wild and passionate. They were all so different and would have expressed the miraculous life of God in their own unique ways.

Miracles are for everyone

When Aliss and I first returned from ministry school, one of our local church leaders was keen to tell us that what we did (meaning the 'power evangelism'), was our unique ministry and not for everybody. I knew what was meant by that, but I felt it was missing the point. It wasn't the way we were doing ministry, it was the fact that we were beginning to see the effectiveness of real spiritual authority that mattered.

Despite the reluctance of some, we were encouraged by many who recognised the real power of God and wanted to see the same in their own lives. There is no 'cookie cutter' way to live and express the 'normal supernatural Christian life', the main thing is that you live it in the way that God has uniquely made you. Jesus said that the power and miracles are for everyone that has the desire, faith and courage to see them (see John 14:12).

Courage is not about having confidence. Courage is about pushing through the doubts and fears and doing it anyway. In the context of spiritual authority, it's putting ourselves into a vulnerable position that is often quite humbling. This is the kind of faith action that seems to place an irresistible demand on the Kingdom of Heaven. In other words, if God doesn't show up there is no 'plan B'. God is attracted to that kind of vulnerability because it gives Him an invitation and an opportunity to manifest His glory.

The Anointing destroys the yoke

We have already seen how the symbols of the bread and the wine in the Communion correspond to the blessings of provision and wholeness. When we take these elements together in remembrance of the Lord's sacrifice it is a powerful spiritual act which releases protection and authority in our lives. I believe the element representing the anointing for power, namely olive oil, is not present in the Communion because the Holy Spirit is present with us. It is through the work of the cross that the Holy Spirit has been poured out on all flesh and it is this that breaks the power of the enemy:

"And the yoke will be destroyed because of the anointing oil." Isaiah 10:27

The yoke in this scripture is a symbol of spiritual oppression and it's through our anointing from the Holy One (1 John 2:20) that this is not only broken, but completely destroyed. Aliss and I have often found that sharing the Communion brings us great strength and encouragement, particularly at times of spiritual attack.

Living a life of faith and courage can be stretching and challenging. This is where we can really help one another, because sustaining a level of motivation to contend for a life like this is tough for most people. We've found that relational support networks are invaluable at providing the mutual support and encouragement we all need for such an aspiration. Similarly, Aliss and I have invested in producing resources that help train others in supernatural living and provide inspiration and support that can help 'kick-start' or catalyse faith for miracles. There are plenty of great resources out there to help you, so get all the encouragement and training you can, and in turn share your challenges, testimonies and victories with others. Let's see 'the normal supernatural Christian life' become a present reality for us all.

The Threefold
Messianic
Mandate

Chapter Thirteen:
The Power of the Spirit

"The Sovereign Lord has filled me with his Spirit. He has chosen me and sent me to bring good news to the poor, to heal the broken-hearted, to announce release to captives." Isaiah 61:1 GNT

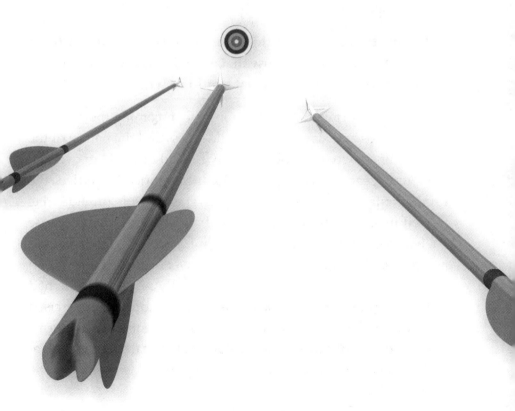

In Luke 4 verse 14 we are told that Jesus left the wilderness in the power of the Spirit. He entered the wilderness full of the Spirit, but He left the wilderness in the power of the Spirit. There is an undeniable connection between what took place in the wilderness and what came after. Jesus as the Son of God did not have to do anything to secure His Heavenly Father's love because He already had it (Luke 3:22). However, Jesus as the Son of Man had to learn and demonstrate obedience to His Heavenly Father (Hebrews 5:8) to operate in legitimate power on earth. What manifested publicly in Jesus' ministry was what had been established personally. What flows through the mouth and hands is what has been established in the heart (Matthew 12:34).

After His victory in the wilderness, Jesus went on to have three years of incredibly powerful ministry on earth, characterised by authority, healings and miracles. So much so, that at the end of John's gospel, we read:

"Jesus did many other things as well. If every one of them were written down, I suppose that even the whole world would not have room for the books that would be written." John 21:25

There is a correlation between Jesus overcoming the curses of lack, sickness and slavery in the wilderness and the nature of the miraculous power that subsequently flowed out of Him over the next few years. Because Jesus had categorically settled the fundamental faith issue of trusting God as His sole provider, He moved in supernatural miracles of abundant provision. Because He had passed the test of trusting that He was wholly loved and accepted by His Heavenly Father, the power of healing restoration flowed out of Him for both body and soul. And because He had humbled Himself under God's word and authority, He exercised miraculous power, not only over natural elements such as storms but also over evil spirits and even death. Let's take a brief look at each of these three areas of supernatural power:

Jesus' miracles of provision

Many of the miracles of Jesus involved the supernatural multiplication and provision of food and drink. In fact, one of the first miracles mentioned in Luke's gospel account after His temptations in the wilderness is an abundant catch of fish:

> " *What flows through the mouth and hands is what has been established in the heart* "

"...they caught such a large number of fish that their nets began to break." Luke 5:6

Just imagine how incredible it would have seemed to those fishermen who had been toiling all night with nothing to show for it, to suddenly have way too much to handle. The excited commotion of people on the shore as they watched in amazement; children laughing and running around, dogs barking and all the while Jesus smiling as He looked at their delighted faces. It's no wonder that Peter fell at His feet and declared, **"Go away from me, Lord; I am a sinful man!"**

The event was so wonderful, they realised this miracle of provision was about much more than simply food and money. When all they ever worked for was in their hands, they discovered that they didn't really want the provision so much as they wanted the provider. And so, everything Simon Peter had ever known was about to turn upside down and inside out:

"Then Jesus said to Simon, 'Don't be afraid; from now on you will fish for people.' So they pulled their boats up on shore, left everything and followed him.'" Luke 5:10-11

Jesus revealed His glory

In the gospel of John we read that Jesus' first miracle was changing 160 gallons of water into fine wine at a wedding in

Cana. John states that this was the first of the signs through which Jesus revealed His glory. In the same way, God had first 'revealed His glory' through the miracle of provision in the wilderness when He fed the Israelites with manna. The Hebrew word for glory here is the same word for 'heaviness' or 'weight'. In antiquity it was a characteristic of affluence and glory to be physically heavy, so it's no accident that glory is often closely associated with food.

When Jesus 'revealed His glory' He was demonstrating that God's Kingdom is manifested through the provision of both physical and spiritual sustenance. The miraculous catch of fish spoke prophetically of the harvest of souls that His disciples would reap, and at the wedding banquet Jesus showed how the new wine of the Spirit would bring great joy to His bride.

All Jesus' miracles of provision seem to be characterised by abundance; the catch of fish that nearly sank two boats, the miracle of feeding 5,000 people with five loaves of bread and two fish. Not only did thousands receive lunch that day but there were 12 baskets of food left over. It's clear that when the abundance of heaven provides, there is always more than enough. The purpose of the miracles was greater than the food itself, it was to lead people to recognise that Jesus Himself was the Bread of Life (John 6:35), the manna from heaven.

True prosperity

There is an undeniable connection here between Jesus' choice to trust God for His provision in the wilderness and the miracles of provision that subsequently flowed out of his life. Jesus demonstrated miraculous provision out of a heart that had settled the issue of who His sole provider was. This is a lesson for every follower of Jesus who seeks to walk like Jesus walked. Material prosperity should never be a goal for a follower of Christ. There are many warnings about the dangers of wealth in the teachings of Jesus. However, prosperity, just like money, in and of itself is not evil, but rather it is the love or worshipping of it (1 Timothy 6:10).

We see that material wealth is celebrated in the Old Testament as a blessing from God by the likes of Job, Abraham and King Solomon. In the New Testament, wealthy women helped financially support the disciples, rich men paid for the burial of Jesus, and trades people like Lydia helped resource Paul's mission. As ever, we must walk the narrow way and find the balance. The Bible teaches that true prosperity is living a life that is full of God regardless of the circumstances. The truth is that real poverty can be having too much to eat and still not being satisfied, or too many material belongings and still not knowing contentment.

Prosperity can obviously be a curse and a snare if it is an idol. But I believe, just like God inaugurated in the Garden of Eden, He does and will bless His children with true prosperity. That's why John writes:

"Beloved, I pray that you may prosper in all things and be in health, just as your soul prospers" 3 John 1:2

The worst kind of poverty is to prosper in all things but our soul. We must come to understand that material provision is not proof of God's blessing, but can be a blessing when placed in the life of a truly prosperous soul. That is the kind of blessing that can spill over and touch a poverty-stricken world.

Healing and the Sabbath

One of the most prevalent characteristics of the ministry of Jesus was His amazing healing power. The gospels are punctuated with story after story of jaw-dropping accounts of awesome healings and incredible statements like this:

> " *Real poverty can be having too much to eat and still not being satisfied, or too many material belongings and still not knowing contentment* "

"Jesus went through all the towns and villages, teaching in their synagogues, proclaiming the good news of the kingdom and healing every disease and sickness." Matthew 9:35

Jesus healed the incurable diseases, the blind, the lame, those who had been suffering since birth and those who had spent all their money on doctors and had just got worse. Though His mission was primarily to the Jews, he also healed Gentiles, the outcasts and the unclean; we might say the good, the bad and the ugly!

As well as His ministry of restoration or building up, Jesus also had a ministry of pulling down. Part of His mission was to expose hypocrisy and tear down ungodly strongholds. He knew His life and message was a direct threat to the religious order and Jesus was particularly adept at making the Pharisees look bad in front of the crowds. They fell into their own traps as they consistently baited Jesus with their rigged questions. One of the acts of Jesus that particularly angered them was His healing of people on the Sabbath. They saw these acts of compassion as 'work' and therefore as acts of blasphemy against God's law. On one occasion Jesus corrected their corrupt understanding:

"Jesus said to them, 'The Sabbath was made for man, and not man for the Sabbath. So the Son of Man is Lord even of the Sabbath.'" Mark 2:27

God had blessed the seventh day and called it holy because He rested on that day and invited creation into His rest. It is an everlasting rest in which creation becomes utterly complete and whole. After the Fall, as we have seen, this unity or wholeness is broken and the law of keeping the Sabbath is given as a guard against the sin of ceaseless toil.

It's no wonder then that Jesus didn't hold back from the work of healing and wholeness on the Sabbath day, because it was made as a time to enter God's holiness and wholeness. A day for restoration and healing. The legalistic and unloving coldness of the Pharisees particularly angered Jesus and in turn He gave them a problem they had to eliminate:

"He looked around at them in anger and, deeply distressed at their stubborn hearts, said to the man, 'Stretch out your hand.' He stretched it out, and his hand was completely restored. Then the Pharisees went out and began to plot with the Herodians how they might kill Jesus." Mark 3:5-6

Jesus' miracles of spiritual authority

And finally, we see that Jesus demonstrated authority on a level never seen before in a single man. Because Jesus had demonstrated absolute submission to His Heavenly Father in the wilderness, He embarked on a ministry of power and authority both in word and deed. It is no small thing that Luke records how Jesus left the wilderness in the power of the Spirit because from this point on in the gospel account, Jesus demonstrated amazing power over both spiritual and natural realms. In Luke's narrative, the very first act of Jesus after His rejection in Nazareth is the casting out of an evil spirit:

"In the synagogue there was a man possessed by a demon, an impure spirit. He cried out at the top of his voice, 'Go away! What do you want with us, Jesus of Nazareth? Have you come to destroy us? I know who you are—the Holy One of God!'

'Be quiet!' Jesus said sternly. 'Come out of him!' Then the demon threw the man down before them all and came out without injuring him." Luke 4:33-35

The people who witnessed these acts were amazed at Jesus' demonstrations of spiritual power. Over and again we read in the Gospels that the people asked themselves, "Where does He get His authority?" and, "Why do the demons obey Him?" Jesus demonstrated authority over the weather with the calming of the storm, over plant life with the cursing of the fig tree, over the fish in the sea, over the waters of Galilee when He walked on the waves, and power over countless demons. Perhaps most significantly, Jesus even demonstrated power to raise the dead, the ultimate act of restoration.

Freedom from sin

What's more, Jesus shocked the religious community of His day by offering freedom from the most terrible captivity of all: unforgiveness. Jesus forgave sins. He came to lift up the face of the condemned and lead them into the light of reconciliation with God. The religious authorities of the day were outraged. In the first place they said, "Only God can forgive sins", a statement which inadvertently revealed the true identity of Jesus. But secondly, they knew that if forgiveness could be granted like this without the need for sacrifice at the Temple, then Jesus was effectively disposing of the need for a sacrificial system. He was putting them out of a job.

The teachings of Jesus were not just empty talk because they were accompanied by real, miraculous power. The forgiveness of Jesus was restorative in every way; the lame would walk and the blind would see as Jesus demonstrated the redeeming nature of His Kingdom's rule and reign. He then taught the people that this was the nature of His Kingdom as He spoke with great wisdom and love. People were amazed at His teaching saying that no man had ever taught with such authority (Matthew 7:28-29).

Temptation at the fall:	Curse released:	Jesus' messianic mission statement (Isaiah 61 / Luke 4):	The Miracles of Jesus:
Good for food	Famine (a lack of provision)	Good news to the poor	Miracles of provision
Pleasing to the eye	Disease (a lack of health)	Heal the broken-hearted	Miracles of healing and restoration
Desirable for gaining knowledge	War (a lack of freedom)	Release to captives and freedom to those in prison	Miracles of deliverance and authority over nature

Chapter Fourteen:

The Wilderness and the Cross

"The law says we are under a curse for not always obeying it. But Christ took away that curse. He changed places with us and put himself under that curse."
Galatians 3:13 ERV

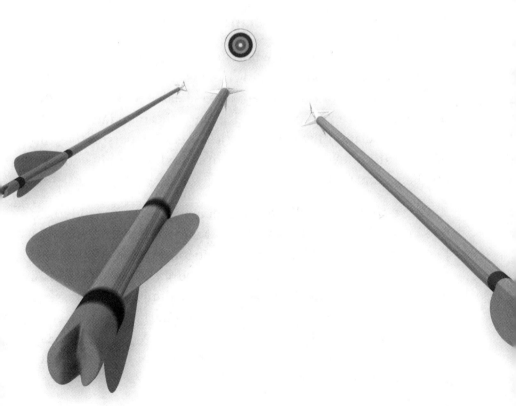

I n considering the miracles that Jesus performed during his earthly ministry, we have arrived at a significant turning point in our threefold journey. Where the first Adam failed in this threefold temptation and released curses, Jesus, the second Adam, was victorious and released blessings. But that is not the end of the story. In many ways, it's just the beginning, because Jesus came not only for His and His Father's sake, but for all mankind (2 Corinthians 5:15).

When Jesus took on the three primal temptations of the devil in the wilderness, He was establishing His messianic identity as the Son of God. He was proving that no matter what came His way He would always do and say what He saw and heard His Father doing and saying (John 5:19). His decisive victory in this 'battle of the ages' became the qualification from which He would go on to fulfil His ultimate mission: to redeem the whole of creation (Acts 3:21).

Jesus proclaims His messianic mission

Shortly after leaving the wilderness, Jesus went on to proclaim His messianic mission by reading from Isaiah 61 in the Synagogue (Luke 4:16-21). From God's eternal perspective we know that this had already been accomplished 'before the foundation of the world' (Revelation 13:8), but from Jesus' earthly perspective, this was a future event to be accomplished through courage, obedience and faith.

We've already seen that this personal victory in the wilderness was instrumental in releasing the power of the Spirit in Jesus' life. Everywhere He went and everyone He touched encountered the provision, wholeness and authority of the Kingdom of God in all its glorious power. But that was only the beginning of His mission. Jesus knew that He had to set his sights on the horror of the cross to **'bring many sons to glory'** (Hebrews 2:10). A unique aspect of Jesus' messianic mission was to be **'the Lamb of God who takes away the sin of the world'** (John 1:29).

Only Jesus as both man and God was able and willing to complete this task. The torture and crucifixion of Jesus is the culmination of Christ's work to reverse the curse of sin and death over mankind. Scripture teaches us that not only did Jesus carry the burden of the curse but became a curse to destroy it completely in His sacrifice (see Galatians 3:13).

During this journey of the blessings of the Kingdom, I have traced the threefold pathway through the scriptural narrative, making a chain reference where applicable. However, what I offer here, particularly as we come to the triumph of the cross, are threads I have caught a glimpse of, but certainly not the whole picture. I offer the following as personal reflections from my own meditations on the cross.

The cross breaks the curse of lack

Of all the cruel and humiliating treatments that Jesus had to endure throughout His mock trial, torture and execution, nothing symbolises the breaking of the curse of lack quite as poignantly as the crown of thorns. In mockery of the accusation that Jesus had claimed He was 'the King of the Jews', **"The soldiers twisted together a crown of thorns and put it on his head"** (John 19:2).

Adam himself had exchanged his 'crown of glory' (Psalm 8:5) for a 'crown of thorns' when he chose to take for sustenance that which was outside God's perfect provision. The resulting curse over Adam was that the ground would produce thorns and thistles for him; by the sweat of his brow he would eat his food (Genesis 3:19). 'The sweat of the brow' is indicative of the thought life because it's the result of man's own labours upon his head or his mind. From this point on, mankind became corrupt in their thinking and it meant that their perception of provision would always be tainted by self-sufficiency. We would subsequently tend to believe that our toil alone was responsible for our security instead of God's gracious provision.

The curse of lack is not merely a lack of physical food, but a state of the heart. It's about anxiety and fear for one's future security. Jesus taught His disciples the folly of worrying about food and clothes and storing up provision for the future. He counselled them to seek after the Kingdom of God and these external needs would be taken care of by their Heavenly Father (see Matthew 6). The curse of lack is primarily about self-centred thinking that seeks first the provision and then the provider. The result of this way of life is a 'crown' or paradigm of 'thorns and thistles'.

The Lord will provide

In Genesis, we read the story of the elderly Abraham and his promised son Isaac. In chapter 22 God tested Abraham by commanding him to sacrifice his beloved son of promise. This is a shocking and dreadful proposal by any moral standard. In this prophetically messianic act we see a father totally committed to unquestioning trust that God would ultimately provide 'the sacrificial lamb'.

The high drama plays out until the last possible moment when, just as Abraham raises the knife for the death strike, God commands him to stop. Lifting his head in fear and trembling, Abraham sees before him a ram with its horns caught in a thicket of thorns. God had provided and the son of promise was secure. Is it possible that as the ram was sacrificed, it still retained a remnant of the thorny brambles around its head?

"So Abraham called that place The LORD Will Provide. And to this day it is said, 'On the mountain of the LORD it will be provided.'" Genesis 22:14

Jesus chose to wear Adam's crown of thorns, not because He deserved it, (because as we have seen, Jesus had defeated the temptation to provide for Himself), but because humanity deserved it. As a son of Adam, Jesus chose to bring the curse of poverty and lack to an end by becoming that curse and taking it down to the grave with Him. The sacrifice of Christ on the cross is essentially an exchange. Jesus died on behalf of Adam's fallen race and paid the penalty for disobedience and sin so that mankind could be declared 'not guilty' or righteous in God's sight:

> " *When Jesus died, He broke the curse of poverty and lack that was unleashed on mankind in Eden* "

"Once you were alienated from God and were enemies in your minds because of your evil behaviour. But now he has reconciled you by Christ's physical body through death to present you holy in his sight, without blemish and free from accusation." Colossians 1:21-22

When Jesus died, He broke the curse of poverty and lack that was unleashed on mankind in Eden. He Himself became lack so that He might be our Bread of Life. The Scripture that follows Jesus' messianic mission statement in Isaiah states **'to bestow on them a crown of beauty instead of ashes'** Isaiah 61:3. Through Christ, the curse of lack and poverty would be exchanged for heavenly provision, a crown of glory; God's glory and honour restored to man.

The cross breaks the curse of sickness

The Roman torture and execution of Jesus involved a horrific flogging which typically consisted of 39 lashes of a cat-o-nine-tails, a whip made up of 9 thongs, often with small pieces of metal tied to the ends to maximise the damage inflicted. This barbaric instrument could effectively remove the skin and flesh from a victim's back in just a few strokes.

This awful punishment is a grisly picture of vulnerability. It's a gruesome representation of mankind's fallen state when we lost God's protective covering and became vulnerable to the sting of sickness and death. Jesus received Adam's humiliation and curse in His flesh so that mankind could once again enter the protective blessing of wholeness.

It is not overtly stated in Scripture how many lashes Jesus would have received under the Roman scourging but we do know that, as far as the Roman Consul Pontius Pilate was concerned, this flogging was supposed to be *instead* of a death sentence. He was trying to spare Jesus and appease the crowds who were baying for His death so it would have been a significant punishment (John 19).

By His stripes we are healed

The cruel irony is that if Pilate had thought he would be sending Jesus to be crucified, it is highly unlikely that he would have ordered Him to be flogged as well; that would have achieved nothing. In the moving portrayal of the crucifixion in the 2004 movie 'The Passion of the Christ', Jesus kneels at the tethering post and as His shirt is torn from His back He looks to heaven and says, 'Father I am ready'. Though not in Scripture, I believe this re-imagining of Jesus' dreadful flogging must have come close to the reality.

Jesus, the One who was whole, offered His back to the teeth of the Roman whip to make those who were broken whole again. Through His nakedness and shame He clothed those in despair with garments of praise and joy (Isaiah 61:3). The prophet Isaiah foretold in startling detail the nature of the Messiah's sacrifice over 700 years before Roman supremacy. As well as the words, **"He was pierced for our transgressions"**, describing death by crucifixion, he also foretold the torture of His flogging when he wrote, **"By his stripes we are healed."** (Isaiah 53:5).

The cross breaks the curse of slavery

Isaiah 53 also tells of the suffering Messiah who was pierced for our transgressions and the punishment upon Him that brought us peace. Jesus as a man was willing to submit to the Holy Spirit whatever the cost and thus moved in great power and authority. In Philippians we read that it was this mindset of humility that caused God to exalt Jesus to the highest place:

"...have the same mindset as Christ Jesus: Who, being in very nature God, did not consider equality with God something to be used to his own advantage... Therefore God exalted him to the highest place..." Philippians 2:6,9

War and conflict are the absence of peace and so Jesus came as the Prince of Peace to end all strife. He came as a servant leader who even washed the feet of His own disciples. The Apostle Paul often refers to God's redemptive plan through the suffering Messiah as 'a mystery hidden before all ages' because nobody seemed to know exactly how the Kingdom would come.

The mindset of the first century orthodox Jew was that the Messiah was coming to re-establish Israel's supremacy in the form of a world empire that would expel the military might of Rome by force. When Jesus told His disciples that He must suffer and die, it should come as no surprise to us that Peter rebuked Jesus for demolishing these exciting aspirations. However well-meaning Peter's kindly rebuke was meant to be, Jesus credited it to His adversary, with an impassioned reply directed at the devil himself:

"Jesus turned and said to Peter, 'Get behind me, Satan! You are a stumbling block to me; you do not have in mind the concerns of God, but merely human concerns.'" Matthew 16:23

This is the only other account in the gospels, apart from the temptations in the wilderness, when Jesus addressed the devil directly. Perhaps this was the 'opportune moment' that the devil had been waiting for after his attempt in the wilderness had failed. What a cunning move to use one of Jesus' nearest and dearest friends to persuade Him from His course through an outburst of human compassion. And we can't help but empathise with Peter since he was all too aware of what crucifixion would mean for his friend and Lord.

> " *Jesus as a man was willing to submit to the Holy Spirit whatever the cost and thus moved in great power and authority* "

A common execution

Jesus was subjected to one of the most debasing executions ever created by man; the Roman crucifixion. The execution was devised to have maximum impact in terms of both suffering and public humiliation. It often lasted for days. It was the ultimate expression of subjugation and terror, often reserved for those who dared to openly rebel against Roman supremacy.

A convict was led through the streets in shame carrying their own means of death, stripped naked, and nailed to the wood through their hands and feet. They were hoisted up for all to see and often suffocated under the weight of their own exhausted body. Though we often see stained glass windows, paintings and movies with romantic music playing, execution by crucifixion is grotesque and barbaric in the extreme. The message that a crucifixion conveyed to the world was undeniable; 'This is what we will do to anyone who dares defy us'.

After the slave uprising led by Spartacus in 71BC, the Roman General Pompey had six thousand survivors of the revolt crucified, with their executions lining over a hundred miles of the Appian Way. That's right, *six thousand* crucified at one time; the senses can barely begin to imagine the horror of a scene like that. I guess what I am saying here is that in many ways, crucifixion was not unusual in Jesus' day; it was a common death for a common criminal who was cheap and disposable.

He became a curse for us

The Jewish Scriptures state that anyone who is hanged from a tree is cursed. The Hebrews did not practice crucifixion but often those who had been executed by stoning would have their bodies hung up as a warning to others. That's why Paul says,

"Christ hath redeemed us from the curse of the law, being made a curse for us: for it is written, Cursed is every one that hangeth on a tree." Galatians 3:13 KJV

It is well to remind ourselves that Jesus submitted to the horrors of the cross freely. I'm not suggesting that He wanted to suffer and die like that; to think so would be absurd. What I am saying is that He wasn't a victim taken by force, but rather, He gave Himself:

"This is how we know what love is: Jesus Christ laid down his life for us." 1 John 3:16

This was not for Himself, because as we have seen, Jesus had proven His own righteousness in the wilderness. He was the sinless man who lived under the Kingdom of Heaven's blessings of provision, health and authority. The Lord's broken body lay in the grave for three days before bursting forth in resurrection glory. The threefold curses of sin and death were now utterly defeated, and it was time to reap the rewards. When Jesus went to the cross He went for us, to reverse the curse for you and me. He became powerless so that we could again have the power and authority over the earth we were always meant to have from the beginning. He took our shackles of spiritual slavery to the grave and destroyed them so that we might walk in the blessing of 'in His image reigning' that our Father God meant us to have (Genesis 1:26).

Chapter Fifteen:

Reversing the Curse

"...how much more will your Father in heaven
give the Holy Spirit to those who ask him!"
Luke 11:13

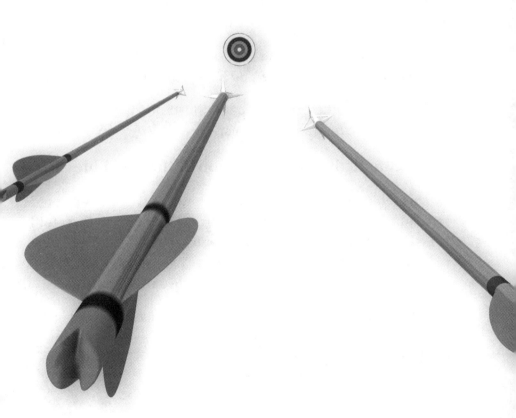

J esus came from heaven to earth (John 3:13) to reverse the threefold curse that Adam and Eve had unleashed through their disobedience. The curse upon humanity was not primarily the manifest presence of darkness but the loss of the manifest presence of God's light. Jesus came to restore that light:

"The light shines in the darkness, and the darkness has not overcome it." John 1:5

He accomplished this restoration of blessing through complete trust and obedience to His Heavenly Father. In turn, God the Father's purpose was to 'seek and save that which was lost' through His son Jesus (Luke 19:10). The curse released by Adam and Eve manifested in a trinity of deprivations we may call famine, sickness and war; they are summarised in death. Through His obedience, Jesus released a trinity of corresponding Kingdom blessings manifesting as the restoration of provision, wholeness and authority; they are summarised as life.

"The thief comes only to steal and kill and destroy; I have come that they may have life, and have it to the full." John 10:10

The table on the opposite page illustrates the relationship between these curses and blessings.

Table chronicling the restoration of threefold blessing

This table recaps the threefold restoration we have explored throughout this book. In the first row, we see the **threefold blessing of God** bestowed on humanity in the Garden of Eden: **provision, wholeness and authority**. These manifest in Adam and Eve's lives as divine **security, acceptance and significance**.

In the next row, we see the **three temptations of Eve** and in the third row, what these temptations were expressing; namely doubt in God's goodness towards them.

| | God's original threefold blessing on humanity: | | |
	PROVISION (security)	WHOLENESS (acceptance)	AUTHORITY (significance)
Temptation (at the fall):	Good for food	Pleasing to the eye	Desirable for gaining knowledge
Sin committed when acted upon:	Doubt in God's provision for me	Doubt in God's love of me	Doubt in God's authority over me
Corresponding curse released:	Famine (lack)	Sickness (disease)	War (slavery)
Man-made hierarchy to compensate:	Economic	Religious	Political
Blessing to Israel symbolised by:	Wheat and bread	Grapes and wine	Olives and oil
Jesus' temptation in the wilderness:	Turn these stones into bread	Throw yourself from the Temple top	Worship the prince of this world
Victory of Jesus in the wilderness:	I trust my God to be my provision	I trust my God loves me	I trust my God in His authority over me
Kingdom blessing re-established (curse reversed):	Provision: miracles of 'more than enough'	Wholeness: miracles of forgiveness and healing	Peace: miracles of authority

The fourth row holds the corresponding **curses that were released** over mankind because of these sins: **famine, sickness and war**. These are not random punishments dealt out by a whimsical god but the consequences of rejecting the divine blessing. They are 'less than' or the antithesis of God's perfect plan.

Next, mankind has built its own **systems of government** to try and counter these curses by their own wisdom: **economic, religious and political**. There is no doubt the world has benefitted in the realms of technology, medicine and agriculture through the work of gifted people. However, these advances have all too often been abused by the few to cause starvation, war and poverty for the many. Flawed by the fallen nature, the paradox is that, **"Thinking themselves to be wise, they became fools"** (Romans 1:22).

Many man-made systems that have aspired to manifest heaven on earth have attempted to ban God from the hierarchy and put ideology as the highest authority (for example, Communism and Nazism). The devastating results of these systems speak for themselves. Over recent times even the private enterprise of capitalism is straining to survive as national debts spiral out of control. Mankind's economic power seeks to provide food and security through business and financial systems, man's religious power seeks to impress God with external control and performance and political power seeks to provide peace through military might.

Next, throughout the Scriptures, we see a benevolent God desiring to **restore the blessings of the Kingdom** to the people of Israel. These blessings are symbolised by wheat fields, grape vines and olive trees. In turn these yield **bread, new wine and olive oil:**

"The threshing floors will be filled with grain; the vats will overflow with new wine and oil." Joel 2:24

And finally, in the last rows, we see how **Jesus fulfilled this messianic prophecy** through immovable faith and trust in His Father's love for Him:

- Jesus conquered any doubt that God will be His provision and He manifests MIRACLES OF PROVISION.

- Jesus eliminates any doubt that His Heavenly Father loves Him and He manifests MIRACLES OF HEALING RESTORATION.

- Jesus conquered any doubt that God alone is to be worshipped and He manifests MIRACLES OF POWER AND AUTHORITY.

For Jesus, all these miraculous manifestations flowed from His immovable faith in His Father God. Likewise for us, all these blessings (both spiritual and manifest), come through personal faith in God, through the one mediator Jesus Christ (1 Timothy 2:5), and lead to eternal life.

> **" *In the trinty of God's blessings there is a virtuous circle of fruitfulness that grows and produces life* "**

Three branches, same root

This threefold branch is a useful model for understanding certain mega-themes within the Biblical account but it's impossible, and ultimately unprofitable, to attempt to separate these elements entirely because they all spring from the same tap root. As Richard Foster points out in his book, 'Money, sex and power': "Throughout history, and in our own experience, these issues seem inseparably intertwined".

True poverty often causes sickness and leads to all kinds of entrapment. Sickness can impoverish and enslave, and slavery is a kind of poverty that causes a malady of the mind and soul. In the grim history of war, some of the greatest killers have been starvation and sickness. The curses of poverty, sickness and war are a diabolical trinity inseparably intertwined. They are the manifest result of the sin nature and they lead to death.

In the same way, just as this trinity of curses is inseparable, it is also true of the threefold blessing. Provision gives us security which enables us to live healthy and balanced lives of purpose and significance. Knowing we are loved gives us the security we need to do selfless exploits and knowing we have a purpose gives us a wonderful sense of wellbeing and affirmation. In the trinity of God's blessings there is a virtuous circle of fruitfulness that grows and produces life.

Threefold blessing flows out of Jesus' life

After Jesus' victory over the seminal temptations of man in the wilderness, He went on to work miracles that manifested the antithesis of each curse. He brought an abundance of food and drink where there was lack, He brought healing and restoration miracles where there was disease. He brought true authority over all the work of the enemy: He cast out demons and commanded the storm to be still and He raised the dead.

The first account of Jesus' acts after He left Nazareth in Luke 4 happen to correspond to these three blessings of His Kingdom:

1. **Jesus drives out an evil spirit. Luke 4:31-36**
   (True spiritual authority)

2. **Jesus heals many. Luke 4:38-32**
   (Healing and wholeness through forgiveness)

3. **Jesus and the miraculous catch of fish. Luke 5:1-11**
   (Provision of food where there was lack)

For the twelve men that Jesus called to follow Him, we can easily imagine how exciting this must have all been. Most had been fishermen by trade and used to the hardworking life of the sea. The physical demands of such a life would have prepared them well for the bodyguard role that the popularity of Jesus no doubt demanded. If someone wanted to get to Jesus, they would have to go through the disciples first.

It must have been exhilarating to be propelled so suddenly from relative anonymity into positions of such significance. Not only this, but in the Jewish culture, to be called by a Rabbi was a mark of great honour. It meant they had been recognised as those with the greatest potential and their destiny was to be like the teacher.

Typically, Jesus' time of ministry (between His baptism and the cross) is divided into three stages, each about a year in duration. These years are progressively described as obscurity, popularity and opposition. His year of popularity (in terms of the masses), was at its height when Jesus fed the five thousand, which is not a surprising outcome when we consider it. But what is surprising is that Jesus seemed to sabotage this popularity on purpose. In John 6 we read that Jesus spoke of the eating of His flesh and the drinking of His blood. This was anathema to the Jewish mindset because drinking blood was absolutely forbidden in the law, let alone cannibalism! And so, we read in verse 66: **"From this time many of his disciples turned back and no longer followed him."**

Jesus asked the twelve if they wanted to leave Him as well. Peter, typically forthright and insightful in his reply said:

"Lord, to whom shall we go? You have the words of eternal life. We have come to believe and to know that you are the Holy One of God." John 6:68-69

From this time on, Jesus would focus His teaching and mentoring, not on the multitudes, but on the few who acknowledged His identity as the Son of God; on those who were not offended by Him. He would go on to teach them about who He was, about His Kingdom, and about how this Kingdom would come through His death and resurrection and the outpouring of the Holy Spirit, the baptism of fire. He would go on to call them, not only servants, but friends; those who would lay down their lives for their Lord and for one another in grace and power.

In Matthew 28 we read the 'Great Commission' of Jesus to His faithful disciples before His ascension into heaven:

"All authority in heaven and on earth has been given to me. Therefore go and make disciples of all nations, baptizing them in the name of the Father and of the Son and of the Holy Spirit, and teaching them to obey everything I have commanded you. And surely I am with you always, to the very end of the age." Matthew 28:18-20

This is a well-known and much quoted passage of Scripture because it often represents what we might call 'standing orders' for all those who have chosen to believe in Jesus and follow His teachings. It's the primary way in which the Gospel and the **'knowledge of the glory of the Lord will fill the whole earth as the waters fill the sea'** (Habakkuk 2:14). The amazing thing about this commission is the premise upon which Jesus bases it. He states that, **'All authority in heaven and on earth has been given to me'**. Think about that for a minute. Did Jesus not have all authority in heaven on the earth before the cross?

To understand this mystery, we must understand that the divinity of the man Jesus was not founded on power but on obedience. That's why we read in Philippians that God **'exalted him to the highest place'** (Philippians 2:9). Jesus modelled true authority for us by modelling true servanthood. The resurrected Jesus was speaking here of the restoration of authority over the earth to all believers, an authority that was accomplished and would continue to be sustained through sacrificial love. The Son of Man (a son of Adam), had now been given the authority over the earth that was lost at the Fall. This meant that the following was now possible: that we could 'Therefore go...'

"...make disciples of all nations, baptizing them in the name of the Father and of the Son and of the Holy Spirit, and teaching them to obey everything I have commanded you."

Do as I do, not just as I say

There are countless sermons written on this commission and most Bible scholars beat a path to the *verbal* teachings of Jesus when considering what this means for us today. There's nothing wrong with that, and we would do well to meditate and aspire to live up to the heady spiritual heights of the Sermon on the Mount. However, when we look at how Jesus really mentored His disciples, a great deal of what He taught them was practical. He wasn't one of those 'do as I say teachers'; He was a 'do as I do teacher'. For example, a major missionary training exercise that Jesus gave His disciples is found in Matthew 10:

"Jesus called his twelve disciples to him and gave them authority to drive out impure spirits and to heal every disease and sickness." Matthew 10:1

And if you think that may have just been exclusively for the twelve, check out Luke 10 when Jesus sends out the seventy two:

"When you enter a town and are welcomed, eat what is offered to you. Heal the sick who are there and tell them, 'The kingdom of God has come near to you.'" Luke 10:8-9

It is evident that when Jesus told His disciples to 'go make disciples and teach them *everything*' that He had taught them, this included *all* that He had taught them to do. Not just the theory, but the practice as well. Furthermore, Jesus told them that those who believed in Him would move in greater demonstrative power than He himself. One of the most challenging verses in Scripture is when Jesus states:

"...the Father, abiding continually in Me, does His works [His attesting miracles and acts of power]... I assure you and most solemnly say to you, anyone who believes in Me [as Savior] will also do the things that I do; and he will do even greater things than these [in extent and outreach], because I am going to the Father." John 14:10-12 AMP

What works did Jesus do? He healed the sick, cast out demons and raised the dead. Who can do these things and greater things? Whoever believes in Jesus as Saviour. How can they do these works? Because all authority in heaven and on earth has been given to Jesus. Why is this so important? Why did Jesus solemnly say that we who believe in Him would also do miracles? Because Jesus came to reverse the curse, not just *for* us, but *through* us as well.

From glory to glory

When we are engaging our faith for any supernatural activity of the Holy Spirit we are participating in the messianic work of reversing the curse:

> " *When Jesus ascended to heaven, His purpose was not to abandon His followers so that things would get worse, but empower them so things would get better* "

"I have given you authority to trample on snakes and scorpions and to overcome all the power of the enemy; nothing will harm you." Luke 10:19

When Jesus ascended to heaven, His purpose was not to abandon His followers so that things would get worse, but empower them so things would get better. John the Baptist tragically began to lose faith in Jesus because he had prophesied that the Messiah would, **'baptize with the Holy Spirit and fire'** (Matthew 3:11), an event John did not witness in his earthly life. However, this prophecy would be fulfilled after Jesus had ascended into heaven and poured out the Holy Spirit at Pentecost (Acts 2).

This outpouring of the Holy Spirit for the baptism of fire has never stopped since. It is the Holy Spirit that gives life to our mortal bodies and His fire that empowers us to fulfil the threefold miracle mandate (Romans 8:11, 1 Corinthians 2:4). Whenever we prophesy by the Holy Spirit, or minister healing or cast out demons we are taking part in a salvific mandate that is deeply grounded in the work of the cross. Jesus' purpose was to reproduce Himself through those who believed in Him and were willing to enter into true discipleship (Ephesians 4:13).

He knew this would bring persecution to many of His followers (John 16), but He also knew that it would bring about a loyal company of people on the earth who would walk in supernatural love and power (John 14:12). The messianic work of Jesus to restore the Kingdom of God in this way is still going on today through all those who are willing to follow.

Chapter Sixteen:
Naturally Supernatural

"Heal the sick, raise the dead, cleanse those who have leprosy, drive out demons. Freely you have received; freely give." Matthew 10:8

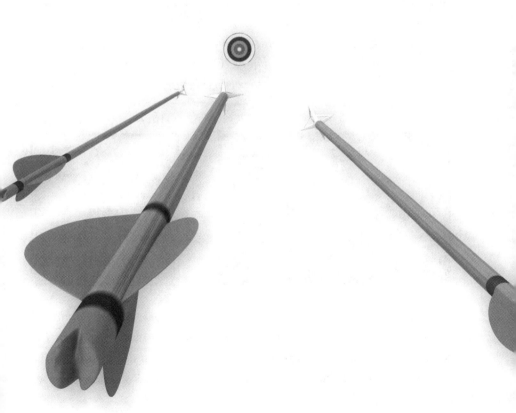

Written below is a small selection of the hundreds of messages we receive from people all over the world whom we've been training to walk in the threefold miracle mandate of Jesus:

"A lady came into our shop in the UK with a cancerous lump the size of an egg in her neck. She was booked in for an operation. We commanded the lump to go in Jesus' name and it began to shrink! We kept praying and when she left the shop it had completely gone. She's been back to the doctor who is amazed. The cancer has left her body and she is completely healed! Praise God!"

"A woman came into our café in Germany who needed an operation to reattach a screw in her knee. She'd previously had an operation to attach a ligament to her leg bone with a surgical screw but it had become detached. It was incredibly painful and she was due for surgery. We prayed for her healing and when she went in for surgery she told them that Jesus had healed her. The doctors laughed at that but when they took a scan of her knee not only had the ligament reattached but the screw and the original hole in the bone had gone! God is so amazing! (PS: Here are the 'before and after' MRI scans to verify this miracle)."

Before: After:

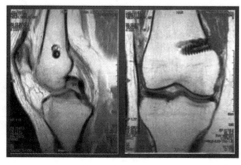   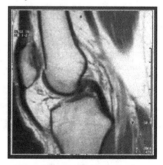

"My wife and I learned so much at your workshop in London. I received an accurate word with direction for my business. Then the following day, after learning how to discern and cast out demons at the workshop, some friends of ours came to our home. We discerned that

they were being affected by evil spirits, so we helped them to get free and then baptised them in our bath tub!"

"I was sitting on an aeroplane across the aisle from a lady who was complaining about a painful neck and shoulders. I offered to pray, and just like Aliss, I just reached out and touched her shoulder and said 'I command healing in the name of Jesus'. She said it still hurt when she tipped her head forward, so I said, 'Let's pray again'. This time all the pain left. She was amazed and kept saying, 'How did you do that? What have you done to me?' I told her God loved her and she said that it was the strangest thing because another stranger had told her that recently in Amsterdam... I think God is on her case! I work in the slums in Ethiopia and I am seeing miracles like this happening all the time now."

"After watching you (Aliss) on TV and reading your books, I immediately received healing in my body. You also encouraged me to step out in faith and miracles broke out. As a result, I quit my job in Australia and moved to the Philippines as a missionary where I have now set up a ministry where we rescue women from prostitution and trafficking and God is moving powerfully."

Aliss and I consider it a tremendous privilege to help train numerous people over the last twelve years through public meetings, books, workshops and more recently online video streaming, DVDs and small groups. Not many of these people are what we might call 'professional ministers'. The majority are from diverse walks of life, all kinds of ages, professions and occupations. For example, estate agents (realtors), nurses, students, chemists, the retired, business people, stay-at-home parents, call centre operators, factory workers, careers advisors, and retailers. Not all start with what we may think of as 'high level miracles', but the important thing is, they are doing it, and as a result people are being saved, healed and delivered. They are stepping out in faith in everyday life, expecting miracles and learning from the Holy Spirit as they go.

My ways are not your ways

At its heart, Christianity was never meant to be an intellectual pursuit. As it first flourished in Europe, Christianity was sustained by those who simply wanted to know and experience God for themselves. From around the 4th Century AD in the west, faith was nurtured in an atmosphere of discipline in monasteries and convents. The goal was not the pursuit of knowledge for its own sake, but edification and worship, contemplation and adoration of God through a lifestyle of devotion.

> *"The Kingdom of God manifests through the most powerful kind of theology; a personal experience of a real and compassionate God"*

This lifestyle was characterised by an expectation and a participation in the supernatural ways of God. The theologian was not a detached observer but a committed involved participant. The highest goal was *personal* knowledge and experience of God. However, by the 11th century, it had become more important to be a philosopher than to be a godly man. Universities birthed scholastic theology whose goal was *objective* intellectual knowledge. Even the idea that one could know or experience God on a personal level began to be challenged.

One of the most liberating revelations I experienced in my faith life was that sharing the gospel didn't have to be an exercise in theological debate. Neither was it something that needed to be staged in a superficial way by an 'organised outreach'. I discovered that with a little discipline and courage, I could prepare daily for divine or supernatural encounters. Here's just one example of how this can happen:

The pink tracksuit

It had become my habit to memorise and meditate on Scripture. Every morning I would recite a passage in my mind and soak in the truth. Then I would open my heart and mind to the Lord and ask him through the Holy Spirit if He had any revelation He wanted to give me about anyone I might encounter that day. On one occasion, I found myself writing down 'pink tracksuit' and 'abdomen'. That was it. I didn't know anyone who wore a pink tracksuit and to be honest I thought it was highly unlikely that I'd meet somebody who did. I was wrong.

That day, Aliss and I met the woman in the pink tracksuit. She and her friend were sitting on a wall outside some local shops and drinking cans of beer. I had just mentioned to Aliss that what I had received from the Lord was a bit random, simply 'pink tracksuit', and to our surprise there it was. We went straight up to them and said, "God told us we were going to meet someone in a pink tracksuit, and he wants to do a miracle in your life!"

We explained that I had received some direction from the Lord in my prayer time and I sensed God wanted to do something about an abdomen area. They were amazed. Her friend blurted out, "We were literally just saying that she needed a miracle! She has a pregnancy crisis and doesn't know what to do". We began to minister to them both and spoke healing and hope into their lives. They had serious addiction problems and all that comes with it. The encounter ended with them kneeling on the pathway, holding hands and asking the Lord to forgive them and come into their lives. They asked for more, so we invited the Holy Spirit to come and fill them, which He did.

This is the kind of encounter that can become a normal part of the believer's life. The only condition is that we 'seek earnestly the spiritual things' (1 Corinthians 14:1 YLT) and that we make ourselves available for them (and 'pursue love'). Within minutes of meeting a stranger on a commute to work or an afternoon of shopping, tears can flow from a timely prophetic word, healing can come through a bold command of faith, powerful ministry and prayer can take place through listening to the Holy Spirit. The Kingdom of God manifests through the most powerful kind of theology; a personal experience of a real and compassionate God.

Chapter Seventeen:
The Threefold Miracle Mandate

"The threshing floors will be filled with grain;
the vats will overflow with new wine and oil."
Joel 2:24

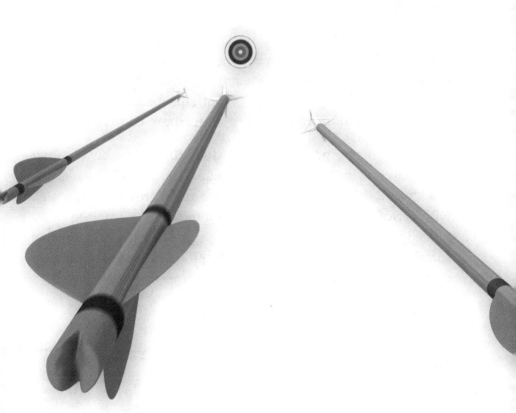

*T*he meeting is on a Sunday within a church building in London, England. There is a small band on the stage leading corporate songs and a presentation screen with lyrics. During the service there is an inspiring talk, a moment of silence and reflection and even an offering.

But this is not church as we know it, this is church without God. Since its launch in 2013, Sunday Assembly has grown to around 70 hubs all over the world, each running weekly meetings[1].

This may sound puzzling to Christians or even shocking at first. The Sunday Assembly's original slogan in 2013 of 'atheist church' was designed to do just that and maximise media interest (it worked). The Sunday Assembly aspiration was, 'We don't do God or religion but we do 100% celebration of life'. They wanted to provide a place of positive social connection that was fun, aspirational and inspiring.

One of the most powerful provocations of the Sunday Assembly to us as believers must be, 'What does church have to offer people then?', since the Assembly, whatever you might think of them, seems to be doing quite well, (perhaps better, in terms of attendance and local impact) than many genuine churches.

Putting it another way, what does the Assembly do that evidently isn't an essential ingredient of church life? They have a weekly gathering, greeters, a live band and a presentation screen with lyrics, an inspirational talk, moments of corporate quiet reflection, community engagement, a variety of philanthropic social schemes, volunteers, free will offerings, funerals, naming ceremonies and wedding rituals... the list goes on.

The purpose of the church

One of the few verses in the Bible that overtly states the true purpose of the church is found in Ephesians:

1. BBC Report 2016

"His intent was that now, through the church, the manifold wisdom of God should be made known to the rulers and authorities in the heavenly realms." Ephesians 3:10

Putting this in context, Paul was saying that the church is the way in which God has chosen to demonstrate His amazing restoration plan through His son Jesus. Wisdom in a Biblical context is always more than intellectual understanding; it's about a reverential and relational knowledge of God:

"The fear of the LORD is the beginning of wisdom, and knowledge of the Holy One is understanding." Proverbs 9:10

Jesus came so that we might not only know this true wisdom but also demonstrate it to others as if it were as obvious as a city on a hill (Matthew 5:14). Manifold means multiple or many and so we see that the divinity of Jesus is revealed corporately in all believers by the habitation of the Holy Spirit. The purpose of the true church is to reveal Jesus (Christ in us, the hope of glory – Colossians 1:27) to the spiritual powers in the heavenly realms.

People of the way

When Christianity first began, it was a radical Jewish sect known as 'The Way' (Acts 9:2) and soon extended to Gentiles (since the Holy Spirit didn't seem to differentiate between them). Believers in Jesus as their Messiah and Saviour gathered in each other's homes as a mutually supportive community, breaking bread and sharing wine together as a symbol of salvation. They also met in community spaces such as Solomon's Colonnade near the

" What really distinguished these early believers more than any other characteristic was the fearfully manifest presence and power of God "

Temple (Acts 5:12) for worship and debate and engaged in good social help programmes such as feeding the poor and caring for widows. However, what really distinguished these early believers more than any other characteristic was the fearfully manifest presence and power of God.

'**The apostles continued to perform many signs and wonders among the people**' (Acts 5:12), but it wasn't just the original disciples. Men such as Stephen and Philip were like human dynamos of the supernatural with miracles breaking out wherever they went. Acts 6:8 says: **"Now Stephen, a man full of God's grace and power, performed great wonders and signs among the people."** And Acts 8:6: **"When the crowds heard Philip and saw the signs he performed, they all paid close attention to what he said. For with shrieks, impure spirits came out of many, and many who were paralyzed or lame were healed."** These guys were waiters serving tables at a Jerusalem soup kitchen, but they were also walking and living in the reality of divine life.

Before the goal of Christianity became an exercise in intellectualism, many saints' lives were characterised by the miraculous. The supernatural resonated around lives devoted to spiritual contemplation and service. Visions, dreams, angels, prophecies and miracles were to be expected by all those experiencing the manifest presence of God.

And so, in what has been described as the 'post-modern age' or even the 'post-church age' could it be that organisations like the Sunday Assembly are a clarion call to abandon 'seeker friendly church' and return to supernatural and risky, even dangerous, church? A people who actually reveal the reality of God in Jesus through the habitation of the Holy Spirit in their lives? A people who walk in the authentic power of the gospel, demonstrating the living power of God wherever they go?

The Threefold Joseph Anointing

In his book, 'Angel's That Gather'[2], Paul Keith Davis tells of a powerful dream he experienced of a sports-like game that culminated in the score between the army of darkness and the army of light being 41:41. Puzzled at this impasse Paul Keith enquired of the Lord the meaning of the dream and was led to read from Genesis 41:41.

'So Pharaoh said to Joseph, "I hereby put you in charge of the whole land of Egypt." Then Pharaoh took his signet ring from his finger and put it on Joseph's finger. He dressed him in robes of fine linen and put a gold chain around his neck.' Genesis 41:41-42

Again, we see the threefold blessing dramatically revealed in the life of Joseph. Having suffered the long years of slavery and lack with humility and fortitude his promotion from prison to palace was dramatic. The signet ring is a symbol of **heavenly provision**, the robes of fine linen of **priestly wholeness** and the gold chain of **royal authority**.

God was revealing through Paul Keith's dream that He was about to manifest this 'Threefold Joseph Anointing' to bring His church into decisive victory in these last days. The story of Joseph reminds us that this threefold inheritance comes through grace (it was his God given destiny), but also through endurance and contention:

"Now if we are children, then we are heirs - heirs of God and co-heirs with Christ, if indeed we share in his sufferings in order that we may also share in his glory." Romans 8:17

Expecting Miracles

We began our journey by asking some basic questions about miracles: What purpose did miracles have throughout the Bible?

2. Angels That Gather by Paul Keith Davis, Dove Company Publishing 2011

What part do they have to play in the Christian faith, and if they do have a part, how important are they in terms of discipleship and salvation?

I hope this book has helped bring clarity to the role of miracles in the believer's life. More importantly, I hope it has brought inspiration and motivation for the role of miracles in *your* life. In the Kingdom of God, miracles are not some optional extra for a few Pentecostal or Charismatic types, and neither are they for some

> " *The public release of true miraculous power is intimately entwined with the private cultivation of devotional faith* "

especially good or gifted people. Rather they are the outward accompanying manifestations of spiritual realities (1 Corinthians 4:20). Miracles are not a 'faith add-on' but an essential unfolding part of God's sovereign work to renew all things through His son Jesus Christ.

Ultimately salvation is simply another word for total healing. When we are saved by the Lord we are rescued, healed and delivered. Essentially, prophecy too is a ministry of healing because it brings the power of God's salvific will to bear. Deliverance too is healing because it sets us free to be restored into the good purposes of God. All these ministries of the Holy Spirit have redemption at their heart.

I am convinced that anybody who believes that Jesus is the Son of God (the Christ) and their personal Saviour can receive supernatural revelation, heal the sick and cast out demons. All that is required is a hunger for the Word of God, a desire to listen to and obey the Holy Spirit and a big dose of courage. The aim is not to become an expert healer or exorcist but to become those who know God and walk in spiritual realities with compassion and grace. We can only start where we are, but the Holy Spirit as our mentor and encourager ever calls us on into the adventures of 'the greater works'.

Private devotion and manifest power

When the disciples began to move in the miraculous, this wasn't something new. It was the ancient power of the Tree of Life that imbued the Garden of Eden with eternal life, love and unity. At the end of the age when Jesus makes all things new, it will imbue the Holy City that shines with the light of God. This is the power that has flowed out of personal devotions of prayer and contemplation towards God throughout the ages.

Through the blood of The Lamb, ordinary people like me and you are being spiritually regenerated into the supernatural human beings we were always created to be. Every day people all over the world are stepping out in faith for the first time and being surprised by God. They are like the disciples coming back from their mission trips laughing and testifying of God's goodness, amazed that even the demons obeyed their commands. And Jesus rejoices with everyone, saying, "I saw Satan fall like lightning from heaven." Luke 10:18

The public release of true miraculous power is intimately entwined with the private cultivation of devotional faith. The personal determination to cultivate a dedication to the Word of God and flow with the Spirit of God results in a life that receives the blessings and releases the power of God. The blessings come from a lifetime of committed discipleship, the power is released in precious moments of glory and wonder.

The MIRACULOUS PROVISION OF GOD is released from a heart that is OVERFLOWING WITH GOD.

The MIRACULOUS HEALING OF GOD is released from a heart that knows it is DEEPLY LOVED BY GOD.

The **MIRACULOUS AUTHORITY OF GOD** in both the spiritual and natural realms is released from a heart that is **CONFIDENT IN THE GOD IT SERVES.**

As we learn to receive the blessings of God through our Sonship, we enter into our divine inheritance to fulfil the threefold miracle mandate and be a people of power.

**"So we fix our eyes not on what is seen, but on what is unseen."
2 Corinthians 4:18**

As children of the promise, we have a glorious inheritance that not only gives us great hope for the future, but the presence and power of the Holy Spirit in our lives today. It's in this new way of the Spirit that we can now live and move and have our being (Acts 17:28). And this is not according to the pattern of the world but according to the one to come.

In this life, just like the first disciples, we too can see amazing healings and restoration. We can see the glory of God made known in the land of the living and see those oppressed of the devil set free. We are destined to be a people of power who are transformed from glory to glory (2 Corinthians 2:18). The messianic mission of Jesus is still unfolding because He has left us a miracle mandate to continue what He started. We too are to walk in the threefold blessings of provision, wholeness and authority that He came to restore until He brings all things to completion at His glorious return. Because, after all, in the Kingdom of God, miracles are not really miracles; they're simply normal life.

Epilogue
Robin of Loxley
The Uprising

"He trains my hands for battle; my arms can bend a bow of bronze." 2 Samuel 22:35

*F*irst light in the King's forest and a doe lifts her head; eyes and ears alert. The sound of wheels, horses' hooves and the clink of iron as a rich man's carriage slowly approaches by way of the bridle path. Doves clatter and flap from the treetops, spooked by the passing entourage. Two horsemen pull the wooden passenger box, another leads the way and two guard the rear. Ready for action in chainmail and metal helms, they ride with one hand on their swords. They are superstitious men and the forest road has a bad reputation. Some say it is haunted.

A half-heard whistle in the woods makes the leader suspicious. He raises his hand and the waggon rolls to a clumsy halt. The captain watches and listens as a bead of sweat trickles down his temple. Nothing. Satisfied, he looks back to wave his men forward when, to his alarm, he realises the rear guards have vanished into thin air. Only their horses are left tearing at the grass. He shouts their names but there is no reply. Just his misty breath and the dead echo of his voice in the trees.

A movement in the forest, the shadow of a man and a cracking twig. The captain yells out, "Who goes there?", and drawing his sword he ventures into the forest to investigate. The flick of a knife on a rope, the whiplash of a branch, and the knight is floored. Men in green garb step forward with arrows drawn, pointing toward his chest. Only two soldiers remain. A glance of agreement and they pull hard on their reigns, a last-ditch attempt to flee with their cargo. But though their horses gallop away, the carriage remains. Quick, quiet hands have untethered their charge. The soldiers leave alone.

A score of men emerge from the trees to surround the abandoned box. They are unkempt and simply dressed but of good heart and health. Knocking on the carriage door, their Chief addresses the occupants politely. "Good morning to you, gentle folk. You do us great honour to pass through our pleasant woodland. What shall we say for this valuable service?"

The passengers are an elderly father and his adult daughter. The old man is afraid but the daughter is feisty and intrigued. "This is the King's *forest, and you shall hang for robbing his Lord" she scowls. "Ahh, you are right my lady, this is indeed the true King's forest, and it belongs to those who truly serve him." And even as he speaks, the forest men relieve the carriage of its rich pickings. Undeterred, the woman points a finger at him, "And who is it that has the temerity to insult a Lord of the Realm?"*

The hooded man doesn't reply at first, but raises an eyebrow as he notices the gold rings on her fingers. He takes her hand in his and declares, "Surely no bauble is bright enough for a lady of such beauty" and removing her jewellery adds, "Especially since they will feed hungry families for many months." With a smile, he kisses her denuded hand and blushing, she looks away demurely. Finally he announces proudly, "Robin of Loxley at your service madam." And with a wink, he is gone.

In the Prologue, we began by drawing a parallel between our spiritual inheritance and the story of Tarzan. John Clayton says goodbye to the jungle. He shaves, dresses in viscount attire and begins to learn the new ways of aristocracy. As he returns to his landed estate in England, I want to switch allegories to another popular story which has likewise captured the imagination of readers throughout the generations. Because when he arrives home, to his surprise he finds that his house is desolate. It's been burned and ravaged by enemies. He is confused and angry. Could it be that Jane Porter was lying to him about his inheritance all along?

The legend of Robin Hood

The legend of Robin Hood has many striking parallels with the predicament we find ourselves in as Christians in this world. After many trials and hardships, Robin of Loxley returns home, but all is not well. Whilst the true king, Richard the Lion Heart, has been absent, the evil Prince John has been busy and established a reign of greed and oppression. Robin discovers, to his great consternation, that his castle and the whole estate of Loxley have been 'acquired' by this usurper. All Robin's friends, family and faithful servants who resisted Prince John's power have been imprisoned or killed.

Robin now has a choice. He can either pledge allegiance to the new 'king' or oppose him. He can either accept a mock version of his inheritance and live in bondage to the Prince, or fight for the inheritance that is rightfully his. It's not an easy choice. The Prince has legions of fighters and his

> " *Our daily choice is to hold fast and remain loyal to the absent King or bow to the pretender* "

reach and influence is strong. Robin knows that to oppose him will be a dangerous move, not only for himself, but also for all those he loves.

This is a powerful metaphor describing our situation as followers of King Jesus whilst living in a spiritually dark world. Scripture teaches us that our true King is away and sitting at His Father's right hand in heaven (Mark 16:19). He told us Himself that He would return to judge the nations and rule the earth (Matthew 25:31). But many in our world say He is dead and never coming back. They have even deluded themselves that there is no such thing as spiritual oppression and darkness. However, as those faithful to Jesus, we refuse to acknowledge the authority of the usurper, the devil, who continues to hold court as the 'Prince of this world'. Our daily choice is to hold fast and remain loyal to the absent King or bow to the pretender.

We must fight for the right

If we ever thought that our threefold inheritance of provision, healing and authority was just going to fall into our laps and the powers of this present world applaud our new-found promotion, we were sadly mistaken. Yes, we have been given an inheritance, but we must also contend for it. That's why many verses in the New Testament exhort us to take courage and stand firm:

"In the world you'll have trouble, but be courageous - I've overcome the world!" John 16:33 (ISV)

Our mission is simple but challenging. We are to be about the true King's business in a world where counterfeit blessings have been established and the spiritual powers aggressively oppose the genuine Kingdom. We are not to be tempted back to the law of the flesh (or we might say, the jungle), though that sometimes may appear easier, but we are to be those who do good (Titus 3:8).

It's this test of courage and loyalty that proves us worthy of our calling. Many may balk at a statement like this because it seems to sound more like works than grace. But the Scriptures are full of exhortations to prove ourselves worthy of our inheritance:

"Walk in a manner worthy of the calling to which you have been called." (Ephesians 4:1)

"Let your manner of life be worthy of the gospel of Christ." (Philippians 1:27)

We should not be confused. We are not talking about God's love here. We cannot make God love us any more or any less (John 3:16). We are talking about His benefits and blessings. Our inheritance is fully bestowed upon us by God's grace, but this requires a response. The Scriptures are rich with stories that emphasise this principle and how important it is to God: Cain and Abel, Abraham and Lot, Jacob and Esau, David and Saul, to name but a few. Yes, God loves us all, but He also strengthens those who value what He values:

"For the eyes of the LORD range throughout the earth to strengthen those whose hearts are fully committed to him." 2 Chronicles 16:9

Gathering to the Lionheart's Standard

Robin of Loxley demonstrates how much he values his inheritance by rejecting compromise and taking a stand against tyranny. This reminds me so much of how we must contend for the promises of God in our lives, even when the enemy seems to have the upper hand. For example, if a healing breakthrough does not seem to be coming as quickly as we'd hoped for, it should never make us conclude that healing is not part of our inheritance. Our inheritance is far more about *who we are* than *what we receive*; it's an issue of the heart.

Robin remains a true Loxley, not because he has a pile of stone and land, but because he values and believes in what it stands for. He knows who he is and refuses to compromise the honour of his house. However, there is a price to pay. This also marks him out in the eyes of the enemy as a serious threat. It puts him on the wanted list with a bounty on his head. If we take this kind of stand we become known by the enemy, we become like dread champions (see Acts 19:15 where Paul is known to the evil spirits).

What Aliss and I have witnessed is that a holy discontent is pervading the church and causing believers to rise up and fight for their inheritance. This is happening on both an individual and a corporate level as we see missional communities getting out of the 'come to us' paradigm and becoming salt and light in their own neighbourhoods. They are being trained 'in Sherwood Forest' to use spiritual weapons and gather enemy intelligence. These weapons of our warfare are rooted in the threefold blessings of God and manifest as supernatural revelation, healing and authority. Knowing the scriptures and the power of God (Matthew 22:29) in both personal devotion and public service is bringing an illuminating witness to an increasingly dark and godless world.

It's time to get mobilised

This is a movement that has been steadily growing and I believe we are at a pivotal time in its growth. It's happening on a bigger scale than we can see because, up until now, it's been happening at a grass roots level and is out of sight. This supernatural uprising is being fuelled by those who are giving their lives, not primarily because they want to receive their own inheritance, but because they want their returning King to receive His:

"I pray that the eyes of your heart may be enlightened in order that you may know the hope to which he has called you, the riches of his glorious inheritance in his holy people." Ephesians 1:18

The truth is that His inheritance and our inheritance are profoundly united. His glorious inheritance is in us and our glorious inheritance is in Him. Many of us have 'put up and shut up' for too long, but we have had enough of the devil's schemes. What our enemy is most afraid of is that we will realise how many of us there are and we will start to connect, communicate and strategise. So long as he can keep us thinking we are powerless and few, he is less threatened.

But our witness is that the people of God are getting mobilised. There is a powerful groundswell building as we begin to take courage and grow up into the fulness of our inheritance. We are becoming a warrior bride fit for her returning King. It's time for us to rise up, receive the blessings of God and release His power. It's time for us to truly walk in the threefold miracle mandate.

Author's Note

W hen you find a key, it may open the door to more than one room. It may open up a room which has several more doors within it, which lead on to other curious and wonderful discoveries. This is how it was with 'The Threefold Miracle Mandate'. One of the many challenges in writing this book was to know which of these rooms to leave closed (for now at least), and which to explore more thoroughly.

I first used the basic threefold teaching for a School of the Spirit meeting in 2014 and it has subsequently matured as I've developed it for our workshops and schools. Aliss has been both my best encourager and my motivational editor and I'm grateful to her and my family and friends for putting up with my threefold musings for the past few years (random exclamations of "Wow! I've just thought of another threefold connection!"), I couldn't have done it without you.

I suspect I will continue this adventure of threefold revelation as it unfolds many more wonderful Biblical truths. My hope is that this book will lead you on your own voyage of discovery into the great blessings of knowing Jesus and depth and power of His wonderful Gospel.

Rob Cresswell
Moravian Falls NC

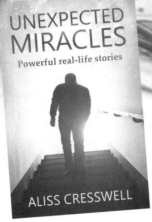